Awakening the Sleeping Tiger Within

Awakening the Sleeping Tiger Within

Breaking the Power of Mainstream Media's
Portrayal of Islam and "The War on Terror"

ANNE MARIE AMERI, PH.D.

ISBN: 1533560838
ISBN 13: 9781533560834

Dedication

I dedicate this book to my children, my heart. I also dedicate this book to all who read it, so they may challenge themselves and benefit from the information, the experiences, the wisdom and thought.

Acknowledgement

I want to thank my editorial consultant, Mr. Robert Weir, for his mentoring, his dedication, hard work and teaching. He took me to the next higher level and I sincerely value his friendship and tenacity.

Memorial

In memory of a 23-year-old brilliant, Lebanese man, Hadi Kasab, finishing his last year of graduate school at Massachusetts Institute of Technology's program, in Computation for Design and Optimization. His advisor Zoltan Spakovszky, professor of aeronautics and astronautics, indicated that Hadi was one of the smartest master's students he had advised. Hadi was working on configuring unconventional aircraft and developing a fast method for computing acoustic shielding of engine noise by the airframe. He developed and implemented new ways to capture the effects of acoustic diffraction and reflection."[1] He planned to graduate in June, 2014, with a bright future. Unfortunately, he was found dead in his dormitory room. Cause of death was found to be cyanide poisoning.[2] May we work together toward never losing another.

Table of Contents

Preface

What is the significance behind the title of this book? Scholars have called Dearborn, Michigan, "The Sleeping Tiger" because that city comprises one of the largest groups of Muslim and Arabic-speaking people in the United States. Among them are many who are incredibly talented, educated, and intelligent. Some are becoming film makers, attorneys, medical doctors, and entrepreneurs; however, not enough are running for political office at the local level. In addition, individuals from this community need to take more assertive and proactive steps to stop negative stereotyping that strategically attempts to define them and lower their morale. This negative stereotyping is rampant in the media and influences Muslim, non-Muslim and non-Arabic speaking society at large.

While Dearborn is one geographic and metropolitan area, I would broaden this description of "The Sleeping Tiger" to include other marginalized groups, including Jewish, nonmilitant

Zionists and non-Zionists. In fact, I am reaching out to all who believe in justice and compassion toward their fellow man.

This book, therefore, is for anyone asking questions and searching for accurate answers about Islam, reasons for negative media coverage of Muslims and Arabs, and a well-documented perspective of how the state of Israel was formed.

Understanding history and the root cause of problems enables us to better formulate solutions. Therefore, in this book, I offer suggestions on how we can help ourselves, support each other, and achieve our true potential by not allowing the current pressures of top tier media and governments to stifle us from reaching our goals.

I will recommend ways we can become more active and contribute more as members of society to serve humankind, regardless of religious or ethnic affiliation. In sum, the goal of this book is to transform any frustrations, fears, and tensions about anti-Islamic, anti-Arabic rhetoric into productive and positive action for the greater good of all humanity.

When I was four-years-old, my astute mother taught me to question what I heard on the news and read in the newspaper. Teaching me "critical thinking skills" at such an early age assisted me throughout my years. With gratitude to my mother, I, likewise, invite you to read this book and hope it will be an informative and provocative source to motivate you to sharpen your critical thinking skills and lead you toward positive action.

Thought provoking questions are asked about issues that are avoided by mainstream media. Throughout this book, I have attempted to be objective, to question, and to discuss issues where only one side has been presented to the public. By activating thought and positive actions, one has the potential to change the fabric of society and improve lives for future generations—not only for Muslims and Arabs but for all people. Although one book can't change the fabric of society, sometimes a small step can be the beginning of an important change.

Born and raised in the U.S., I know and have experienced aspects of the U.S. that are not possessed by many other countries: its excellent higher education system, superb medical care, freedom of movement, opportunity, freedom to practice religion, and an objective and fair civil court system. For the most part, citizens are physically safe from harm.

It is understandable how discrimination in any country can make individuals or groups feel rejected. That rejection may result in depression and later that depression could turn to anger. Instead, I believe that anger can be a motivator for constructive outlets, not terror, oppression and war.

Also, I understand how belonging to any religion may color a person's view of the world, especially if people in your religion have a history of being discriminated against. It is actually easier for a person to become nationalistic, wanting a country, and fighting for a country that you can see and touch. Nationalism is concrete, whereas a religion is usually more conceptual.

When a group fights for domination and entitlement for whatever stated reason, I believe one underlying motivating factor is fear. I am in no way excusing the behavior and atrocities, just attempting to make sense of it. It seems as if these powerful groups and people will perform an action "by any means necessary" to forward their agenda.

This book honors Christians and their religion, those who follow Judaism and their religion and Muslims and their religion. My aim in writing this book is to spread knowledge about right wing militant Zionism, as differentiated from Zionism in general and Judaism, in particular.

After reading this book, it is my desire that analysis and truth seeking will be the first step toward dialogue with others who may have differing opinions. Through dialogue perhaps we can become more understanding and empathetic. And through empathy may we find peace.

I have read about many good-hearted and compassionate people across all religious and international boundaries. They are heartbroken by the effects of the Syrian, Iraqi, and Libyan wars. These victims number in the millions and are, in large part, innocent children and civilians. In fact, the ones who are suffering did not cause the problem. They are, however, paying the price of the wars. On the other hand, there are major grassroots efforts in many countries, led by compassionate citizens to help these refugees, even though their respective governments may not offer much or any help.

It is my desire to motivate adults, youth and future generations to become more critical of the media and the process it uses to distort information about them and their history. Through reflection and critical thinking, people can begin to understand the reason they are maligned and pressured. All of us can learn from the analyses and recommendations in this book to proactively deal with these pressures and exploitations and perform our civic responsibility.

In addition, when thinking about people with differing viewpoints, I do not deny that one can support the interests of the state of Israel while also having compassion for the plight of the Palestinian people. However, I abhor the support of the occupation, the apartheid conditions, and the daily unequal treatment the Palestinian people endure.

To attain peace in the Middle East, we must not make Israel a monster. Israelis, just like any other people, are a heterogeneous group composed of individuals with individual hopes, beliefs, and ideologies. It is also important to distinguish between the political ideals of a state government and the people who may or may not support those ideals. Just as less than 99.99% of Muslims are not terrorists—and indeed most terrorists are not Muslims—we must never over-generalize by condemning all Jews or even all Israelis as Arab-hating Zionists. Further, Zionism finds most of its political and financial support from sources outside of Israel.

We must also remember that Judaism and Zionism are two very different entities. To make my intentions clear, I have a great deal of admiration and respect for the Jewish religion and have close Jewish relatives who I love very much. Similarly, I was raised in a majority Christian society and feel these people are my family. My nuclear and extended family is mostly Muslim, and I am in awe of how many wonderful and kind Muslims I have been privileged to call family and friends.

For sixty some years, I have lived among Arabs and Muslims and have found them to be honest, welcoming, generous, law-abiding, and God-fearing. If they have one negative quality, it is their passivity. How else can you explain allowing negative media, supported by investments of millions of dollars, to bombard and besmirch their religious and cultural character? If Muslims were more proactive and assertive, the people and organizations who besmirch the character of Muslims would be held legally responsible for their ethnic intimidation.

As we reflect upon the current political situation in the U.S. and the Middle East, we can question whether it is really "religion" that contributes to the tragic situation in our world, primarily in the Middle East. Instead, we can easily see that the problems are actually caused by power, control, and greed from some who control corporations and the commercial media industry.

It is my vision that any political, religious or nonreligious groups that are unrepresented or under-represented can benefit from accurate information and the suggestions offered in this book which attempts to cover topics that have many layers of complexity. Therefore, I offer information, reflection, and suggestions both from my range of expertise as a psychologist and researcher and from many others who have a multitude of areas of expertise.

My goal is that readers will have a better understanding of the following areas:

- Arabs and Muslims will have increased awareness of their situation and take additional positive and peaceful action to assert themselves.
- Arab and Muslim parents will better educate their children and youth about their rich heritage and Islamic religious beliefs.
- Arab and Muslim youth will become aware and watchful for ploys by undercover agents to draw them into illicit acts that could be labeled as terrorism, whether by pretending to befriend them personally or through social media.
- Israelis, Americans, Jews, and Christians will understand and become more accepting of Arabs and Muslims as opposed to either benign tolerance or discriminatory attitudes toward them and their beliefs.
- All readers will become aware, if not leery, of the divisive characteristics of top tier mainstream media and understand the reasons for it.
- The similarities between Islam and Judaism will be understood, including the present conflicts that have nothing to do with religion, and everything to do with

the politics of right wing militant Zionism and Western Colonialism.

- Develop a basic knowledge of the turmoil that militant right wing Zionism causes the Palestinians.
- Become knowledgeable about the huge amount of foreign aid the U.S. government is giving to Israel every year.
- Realize there are reports from eye witnesses that indicate that Israel is collaborating with rebel groups inside Syria to fight the Assad regime. (The mainstream media does not publicize this fact.)
- Understand that when propaganda is exposed, it essentially becomes ineffective, over 90% of the time.

Hopefully, this book will make one small contribution to help people of conscience begin their conversation. With that said, we need to begin asking critical questions about everything we read, hear, and see.

Section I

STATEMENT OF THE PROBLEM AND
ACCURATE DEPICTION OF ISLAM

One

Identity Theft

As the words "Muslim" and "terrorist" began to become associated in the media, I had a recurring dream of my purse being stolen, which I interpreted to be a metaphor for my identity being stolen. After the Arab-Israeli War of 1967, I listened to radio broadcasts that said "Palestinians" were "terrorists." I thought, *"How absurd to take an entire group and cast them out of society."* Twenty years later, the media was calling "Arabs" terrorists and now, not surprisingly, the media is terming "Muslims" terrorists.

Trying to cast the world's second largest religious group as terrorists is ludicrous. The motive is political and is used as a rationalization for power, land grabs and greed. This strategy is used to put Muslims on the defensive. We tend to absorb whatever toxicity we hear or see in our environment or in the media, and this toxicity becomes part of us. Constant negative feedback about our identities can affect our subconscious and unconscious minds as well as the attitudes of the general public.

If we accept the *untruth* that we are untrustworthy and not entitled to equal rights, then we could become passive, discouraged and resigned to whatever happens to our situation and to us. Instead of trying harder to achieve the goals that we desire and are entitled to, we could become depressed and give up.

Do you think that Muslims and Arabs should desire social validation in a society where the powers that have control are willing to expend tremendous amounts of money and energy to see that we do not achieve social validation? Of course, we should not. So consider this thought from your personal point of view: If *you* feel alienated from yourself, then you are also alienated from society, and you become increasingly vulnerable to manipulation, particularly through propaganda and indoctrination.

It is an important fact to realize that, if we allow another person or group, such as the media or government, to dictate or define who we are, then we effectively concede our power to someone else. It is even more important to realize that *you* are the only person who is and should be capable of defining your identity.

If someone has an issue with your identity, you must confront that attitude instead of internalizing it. Your demonstration of strength and confidence will earn people's respect. When you stand up for yourself in a logical and unemotional way, the bully who confronts you, usually backs down. Also, becoming an active participant in your chosen cultural or religious group will help you feel accepted and supported.[3] Distancing yourself from your cultural and religious group has the opposite effect.

According to Imam Ali, (cousin and son in law of Prophet Mohammed)

> Your remedy is within you, but you do not sense it.
> Your sickness is from you, but you do not perceive it.
> You presume you are a small entity, but within you is enfolded the entire Universe.
> You are indeed the Evident Book, by whose alphabet the hidden becomes manifest.
> Therefore, you have no need to look beyond yourself.
> What you seek is within you, if only you reflect.
> —Source: *Nahjul Balagha* (Peak of Eloquence)

To put this book in perspective and help see the big picture, let us look at the forces controlling the media. First, understand that these forces engage in "groupthink" or the "them vs. us" philosophy. The mainstream media counts on most people being conformists and not using critical thinking skills.

Many examples will be presented that show how the characterization of our history has been distorted. The pressure and tension felt by Arab and Muslim communities, as well as African American, Mexican, Latino and Jewish communities is not an accident. When top tier media attacks and denigrates entire groups of people because of the actions of a few trouble-makers, we must ask ourselves who is financially backing the perpetrators of these baseless attacks upon so many? They are defiling humanity for their own unjust purposes.

Just as the "War on Drugs" resulted in the destruction of a portion of the African American community, putting many of their young men in prison, the "War on Terror" is destructive to the Arab and Muslim communities. One reason is fear that Muslims or other minority groups are rapidly increasing and could be capable of changing U.S. policies to be more balanced toward Israel.

Once we realize that we have the right and duty to be proud of ourselves and our heritage, we can move toward empowering ourselves and others by accurately spreading the word, running for political office, and working with others to develop and purchase media outlets to make them more balanced and truthful. Let us take the first step to accurately spread the word.

Two

Propaganda

"I have traveled across the length and breadth of India and I have not seen one person who is a beggar, who is a thief; such wealth I have seen in this country, such high moral values, people of such caliber, that I do not think we would ever conquer this country, **unless we break the very backbone of this nation, which is her spiritual and cultural heritage** and therefore, I propose that we **replace her** old and ancient **education system, her culture**, for **if the Indians think that all that is foreign and English is good and greater than their own, they will lose their self-esteem**, their native culture **and** they **will become what we want them, a truly dominated nation.**"

Anne Marie Ameri, Ph.D.

Propaganda is used to keep people isolated and silent. When youth, especially, feel unaccepted and unacceptable, they will spend their time, money, and efforts attempting to prove they are acceptable to the larger society. Youth is a time in life when they particularly want and need to feel accepted.

Minority groups also can easily be manipulated especially when they are unaware of their own proud history. When people know their culture, their history, and their proud identity, no one can make them feel inferior. It is not difficult to Google, "Islamic historical and courageous figures in contemporary society," leaders such as Gamal Abdul Nasser of Egypt, Mohammed Mossadegh of Iran, and Habib Bourguiba of Tunisia. This simple action can result in making one proud of being Muslim. One can read Martin Luther King, Nelson Mandela, J. F. Kennedy, Gandhi, and many others to be proud of your racial, national, or religious group.

Each minority group needs to learn about its history in order to be proud of its identity. (Please see the Chapter on Recommendations for Broader Engagement and Diversity and the Appendix that includes Two Speeches; one by President John F. Kennedy welcoming President Habib Bourguiba of

Tunisia to the U.S. and the second, which is Habib Bourguiba's speech to unite his Muslim and Arab brothers and sisters delivered in Jericho, Palestine, in 1965.)

Ask yourself, "If I were not negatively influenced by the media, what would I be interested in doing? What would I think of myself?" Instead of wasting your time and money on video games, alcohol, and drugs, wouldn't it be more helpful to learn about your history, your roots, and your role models? To reach your important long-term goals, wouldn't it be a better use of your time to formulate strategies, join supportive groups, and become an active member of your community? If you do, then you will be talking and connecting with people who know and care about you and your interests. You will also feel a sense of closeness and being understood.

Do not expect fairness in the top tier media and do not believe most of what you hear and see there. Check the facts by using different sources. When you hear information in the media, ask yourself, "Where is the proof that this information is accurate?" Use your computer to help you find information (but be cautious about using the internet because at times this data could be fabricated as well).

Ideally, media is supposed to disseminate accurate information. But, before you believe any source of information, ask these important questions: "What is the media presenting? How is the media presenting the information? What is the media focusing on and what might be the motivation or 'hidden agenda' for the information? What is the media omitting?" For example, when the media continually broadcasted that nearly 300 schoolgirls were kidnapped by an Islamic terrorist group in Nigeria in 2014, they omitted any acknowledgement that 5,000 Palestinian prisoners in Israel were detained without a court date, many of whom were on a hunger strike. In 2015, when "settlers" in Israel burned a home with a Palestinian family inside,[5] or in 2015,[6] and 2016, when hundreds of Palestinians and Jews in Israel demonstrated together at a checkpoint or highway to end the occupation,[7] this information was not broadcast in top tier media. By comparing media sources and observing the type of information that is broadcast as opposed to the type of information that is withheld in top tier media, one can conclude that the groupthink of top tier media is "divide and conquer" and "lives of one side matter above the other."

A. Inconsistencies in Propaganda

Propaganda strongly emphasizes to the public that Americans should strive to become independent while, in contrast, those in power work together (that is interdependence). In fact, the only way to create change in the system is to work together.

Propaganda focuses on keeping the American public concerned about equality for sexual issues while overlooking equality with regard to religious, national, and racial issues. Although people in other countries realize that their news outlets are the propaganda arm of their government or those who control the government, people in the U.S. are lulled into thinking we can believe information we hear on the news; this is due to the so-phisticated manner of media manipulation. For example, consider CNN's self-promotional claim to be "The Most Trusted Name in the News."

Important questions to ask about propaganda are: its motivation, its purpose, its effects, its goal, and how listeners can respond to broadcasts. The motivation for propaganda is domination to keep certain individuals or some groups in society ineffective and reduce or eliminate their power. Especially in the post 9/11 atmosphere, propaganda serves to alienate Arabs and Muslims by treating them as outcasts or "the other." This makes individuals feel like outsiders who, then, expend a great deal of effort trying to fit in to be accepted by "American" culture. Instead of working to achieve their long-term goals, many of our youth are turning to negative coping mechanisms such as drugs and alcohol as forms of social anesthesia.

Another purpose of propaganda is to hijack the individual's identity by creating an internal conflict. Because each of us grew up with a certain set of values, principles, and character, when we are no longer in control, we become our own worst enemy because we are in conflict with ourselves.

Therefore, the intent of propaganda is often to demoralize us, to strike at our identity, to make us feel "less than" we truly are, to cause "self hatred," and to impose a new identity that will meet the strategic manipulation of "groupthink." Consequently, the demoralized person within the "out" group will not have the motivation to attempt to maximize his or her human potential and often settles for a lower standard of education, employment, and status. Subsequently, this person will probably become a follower instead of a leader and allow the dominating force to impose a false identity onto him or her.

An additional purpose of propaganda is to distract the American public from the truth. While some pro-Israeli groups keep public pressure on Arab or Muslim populations, the wider American public is duped into not concentrating on—nor even knowing about—the billions of dollars given to the State of Israel by the U.S. government every year.

In the meantime, infrastructure in our U.S. cities is allowed to become outdated and often times crumbling. As a result, we see some highway bridges collapse and urban revitalization programs go unfunded. In Michigan, one in four children is living in poverty. In fact, the residents of Flint, Michigan were unknowingly drinking water tainted with lead after state government switched their water source in 2014 in an effort to save money due to Flint's dire financial situation.[8] Despite our sad situations that need urgent financial help and attention, right wing militant Zionists use distractions so U.S. citizens don't focus on the exorbitant amount of money the U.S. is sending Israel each year, instead of financially caring for our own citizens.

Intellectuals including Noam Chomsky assert that you should ask the question, "Is indoctrination or propaganda essential to democracy?"[9] How does a powerful minority get its majority to submit? "To get the majority to submit, you need to control what people think." Chomsky believes that power in the U.S. is becoming consolidated in the hands of a smaller minority. To counteract this, the majority needs to become active in order to build bases for popular movements. Chomsky states that if a society is only concerned with material gain, that society will destroy itself.[10]

B. Spreading Untruths about Islam

To distract the American public who may be unaware about Islam, the right wing militant Zionists invent scandalous propaganda against Islam. They spread untruths, falsify definitions of words and concepts from the Quran, and present myths about Islamic history and how Islam was spread. Let us look at a few examples of these distortions in definitions and untruths: Islamophobia, Jihad, Sharia Law and Terrorism.

1. ISLAMOPHOBIA

Reflect and ask the reasons why hundreds of millions of dollars are spent every year in propaganda toward fueling Islamophobic ideology. Islamophobia, as presented in the media, is defined as the "fear of Islam." The word "Islamophobia" actually means the *irrational* fear of Islam. If "Islamophobes" were actually afraid of Islam, they would stay away from anything having to do with Islam because of their fear. However, this is not the situation whatsoever. A more accurate term for the messages disseminated by the media would be "anti-Islam" or "anti-Islamic sentiment." Because of this anti-Islamic sentiment, Muslims are aggressively provoked. One can notice evidence of this: many mosques in the United States and United Kingdom have been attacked; senseless murders of Muslims have occurred; insulting advertisements are posted in New York subways and on the outside of buses; and there has been a great deal of anti-Islamic rhetoric in the media and even from some candidates hopeful of winning the nomination for U.S. President in 2016.

As mentioned earlier, this sentiment may be happening for several reasons. The first may be that Islam is perceived as a threat because it is not possible to bribe a true believer who submits to God. Second, it is a well-known sociological fact that when economic conditions worsen, the strongest economic groups exert more pressure on the weaker groups, who are often victimized. Third, many right wing militant Zionists want to permanently dislocate Palestinians from their land in Israel and remove them from their rightful homes. This right wing militant Zionist ideology is generally not accepted by Arabs nor Muslims. Thus, some powerful and politically motivated groups and individuals seek to reduce the political power of Muslims and demoralize Muslims in the U.S. and elsewhere in order to control the masses through public opinion.

Hence, top tier media does not give viewers or readers a true reflection of Muslims and Arabs but rather tells audiences how to perceive Muslims and Arabs. The American public only hears one voice and it is not a balanced or fair one.

These anti-Islamic groups scheme to present a biased and inaccurate depiction of Islam in order to create an environment where people simultaneously frown upon and are angry and fearful of Islam and Muslims. Consequently, the general public, ignorant of the truth, may begin to believe that Muslims are inferior, untrustworthy or worse. As a result, the Muslim youth who want to acclimate to Western society, such as those who live in the "sleeping tiger" community of Dearborn, and especially ones who have no accurate information regarding their religion, may begin to feel demoralized and depressed.

The goal for those with anti-Islamic sentiment is to solidify their political gain. Many Muslims, however, as well as others, don't understand the ideology of Islam, its proud history, or its many heroes. Too often, this history has been intentionally hidden. Thus, the Muslim youth who have no knowledge about Islamic history and culture from home or school, and have no idea about the exceptional history of Islam and its historic and contemporary heroes, can become easily manipulated.

When one understands that many history books are written by mainstream authors or the victors, then one understands the reason much of our history has been hidden from us. That is you can easily be manipulated to think the group in power is superior and you are inferior. When you feel inferior, the powerful group begins to dictate how you should feel about yourself and how you should think about your identity. Consequently, if you become depressed and give up achieving your goals, then the powerful group has won because you are one less person who will negatively impact their political agenda.

2. JIHAD

The word "Jihad" is incorrectly used by the media, to spread an untruth that Islam is a religion of violence. This misinformation about Jihad is broadcast quite often in the media today. The word has been inaccurately defined and, by no means, reflects that Islam is a religion of violence. In contrast, the word itself mean "struggle," "striving," or "endeavor," words that, in context, represent our spiritual association with God.

Jihad also has a differentiation between *minor* and *major* Jihad. This fact is apparent by a remark made by Prophet Mohammed early in 600 A.D., after the Muslims won a conflict with the pagans and were returning home to their community. Prophet Mohammed told the army, "You have now won the '*minor* Jihad,' but you still have to win the '*major* Jihad'." What does "*major* Jihad" mean? It means, the *inner* struggle that each of us encounters every single day of our life in regard to situations that arise from our relationships and social interactions or from our mental discourse or conflict when having an internal debate with ourselves.

Whenever we ask ourselves, "Is this the right thing to do or should I do that?" "I know it's the wrong thing to do, but I still want to do it," this is our internal struggle. These thoughts don't have any relationship or bearing on what anyone else thinks of us. Instead, these thoughts are a direct communication within your own mind; between yourself and God or between your desiring self and your wise self.

Instead, our thoughts might be, "Are my decisions and actions correct in God's eyes or not? What will God think of me, and inevitably, what will I think of myself, if I do this or do not do that?" In other words, by focusing on God and reminding ourselves that "God is closer to us than our jugular vein," and that God is with us, at all times, we strive to overcome our rebellious nature. One definition of *Major* Jihad is incarcerating the ego.

According to an interpretation of the Quran by two translators, Pooya Yazdi and Ahmed Ali, there are actually four different types of Jihad: First, the struggle or striving with one's rebellious self, the *Greater* Jihad; second, spending one's wealth in the way of God, to help the poor; third, spreading knowledge for the benefit of those who need it without any thought or expectation of worldly gain or remuneration. Fourth, fighting only in defense of truth, or the truthful, Islam (all those who believe in one God), that includes Christians and Jews as well as Muslims. This last type of Jihad is allowed only under the condition that it is unavoidably necessary to defend the faith, the lives and faith of other monotheistic believers, or one's own life. This Jihad is understood to be fighting in "self defense."[11]

Propagandists misuse the term "Jihadist" to inaccurately describe a group of violent Muslim "terrorists." This is a misnomer because Islam strictly prohibits violence against innocent civilians and has strict rules for warfare. Rules of engagement in war include: trees must not be cut down, water supplies are not to be polluted, and women, children, and missionaries are not to be hurt. Anyone hurting innocent civilians might label themselves as Muslims; however, they are definitely not following the true tenets of Islam.

3. SHARIA LAW

The third untruth is that Muslims living in the U.S. or any other Western countries will impose Sharia Law. The top tier media want the U.S. citizens to be afraid that the Muslims will usurp U.S. laws and impose their own laws. Sharia Law is just another term for religious law. Just as the Ten Commandments are part of Jewish and Islamic Law. According to the Islamic religion, Muslims are to follow the laws of the country where they live. Muslims do not impose their own laws on their host country.

4. TERRORISM

The fourth untruth is that "Muslims are terrorists," which implies that *all or most* Muslims are terrorists. This could not be further from the truth, when 99.99% of Muslims are peace loving and abide by the laws of their respective countries. The statement implying that all Muslims are terrorists is as false as implying that *all* Christians or all Jews or all Hindus are terrorists or violent. Propaganda that spreads the untruth of Muslims are "terrorists" is a manipulation to keep Muslims and Arabs on the defensive and to alienate them from their respective societies.

The reason opponents of Islam claim that Muslims are "terrorists" is because they perceive Muslims and Arabs to be a threat. Right wing militant and political Zionists are afraid of Muslims. The Quran states that arrogant unbelievers (pagan materialists) are more afraid of Islam than they are of God. In other words, saying that Arabs and Muslims all engage in "terrorism" is an attempt to silence their dissident voices.

Consider the fact that Zionists in the U.S.; starting in the 1930s, had U.S. front groups who put up a "false front" or façade in order to hide their own agenda — for their own paramilitary groups in Palestine. In other words, the Zionists created front groups for their own group of "terrorists" in Palestine.[12]

Zionist front groups or paramilitary groups were very effective. Consequently, when Menachem Begin, member of the Irgun (a proclaimed "terrorist" group), and later, Prime Minister of Israel, was asked by Russell Warren Howe during an interview, "How does it feel to be the father of terrorism in the Middle East?" Begin added, "In all the world."[13] The fact is that Begin led the militant Zionist organization that bombed the King David Hotel, attacking the British Mandate government of Palestine and its armed forces in July 1946.[14] Begin was actually bragging that he was the father of terrorism in the entire world!

Another ultra-Zionist, Rabbi Meir Kahane, was the founder of the Jewish Defense League (JDL) in the U.S., deemed by the FBI as a right wing terrorist group in their report "Terrorism 2000/2001". The Southern Poverty Law Center stated that the

JDL preached a violent form of anti-Arab, Jewish nationalism both domestically and abroad. They threw fire bombs at opponents' buildings, vandalized and even planned to bomb the King Fahd Mosque in Culver City, California.[15]

Former President Jimmy Carter's op-ed piece in The Boston Globe, in December 2006, summarized some major points in his book *Palestine: Peace Not Apartheid*. He elaborated, "For 39 years, Israel has occupied Palestinian land, and has confiscated and colonized hundreds of choice sites. Palestinians have been severely dominated and oppressed, often excluded from their former homes, land, and places of worship."[16] Does this shed some light regarding who some terrorists are?

Militant Zionists who use fear-mongering tactics to defame the image of Muslims as terrorists are actually afraid that their own status quo of power will diminish. They see the possibility that organized and educated Muslims, especially in the U.S., may enable Muslims to gain more political power. Militant Zionists also know that Islam is attracting followers at a faster rate than that any other religion. In fact, a report by the Pew study, published by *CNN* in April 2015 states, "Islam, the world's fastest-growing faith, will leap from 1.6 billion (in 2010) to 2.76 billion by 2050." Christianity is also expected to grow but not at the same rate and, by 2050, "for perhaps the first time in history, Islam and Christianity would boast roughly equal numbers."[17]

Groups who favor the Israeli occupation of Palestine believe that by labeling Muslims and Palestinians as "terrorists," these people will be discredited. Consequently, the powerful groups who are presently in power will be able to maintain their positions and take any action to harm people who oppose the occupation. They are afraid of Islam's potential political power as well as the potential power of thoughtful, intelligent, Jews, Christians, and others of conscience in the U.S. and elsewhere.

Language usage is very important in promoting agendas. We are beginning to understand the reasons Muslims and Arabs, the vast majority of whom have never committed an act of violence, nevertheless are labeled "terrorists" in the news media and in everyday conversation; on the other hand, the "occupiers", "colonizers" or the "paramilitary" who usurp Arab land and have no right to it, are termed "settlers." This is a clear example of how language is used to justify oppression and xenophobia.

Why does the U.S. administration agree with Israel every time a resolution is brought before the Security Council at the U. N. whether on the side of justice or not? The U.S. has agreed to politically support Israel at the U.N.

The militant Zionists fear that Muslims may obtain political power, and from their perspective, that fear is real—and rational, not *irrational*. If Muslims were able to obtain political power in the U.S. and change public opinion and government policies to be more fair and just toward Palestine, what would happen to Israel, in its present form? The militant Zionists understand that if U.S. financial support and defense are reduced, as well as no longer counting on 100 per cent support at the United Nations, Israel, in its present form, could not be maintained. Perhaps, one could predict a kinder and more just Israel that would have to maintain peace with its neighboring countries.

These are some reasons right wing militant Zionists feel it is imperative to stifle accurate information in the news media, on college campuses, and other public forums, such as the New York City subway walls, as well as penetrate Hollywood movies and the entertainment industry with anti-Islamic propaganda. They seek to present a biased, one-sided view to U.S. citizens and others around the world in order to hold on to their power and the status quo.

These are a few inconsistencies that we can now begin to question. Look beyond the propaganda, reflect deeply, and then follow your own conscience about truth in the Middle East.

Do the right wing militant Zionists have any thoughts about treating Palestinians with dignity, respect and fairness or to help them economically? What term is used for a country with separate roads, separation wall, and separate treatment for Palestinians?

We realize that Zionists have the power, money, and the latest scientific advancement in physical protection. So, ask the question, "Why would Israel have any incentive to formulate a reasonable peace proposal based on justice with the Palestinians?" According to the current world paradigms to hold on to power and control, at whatever the cost, the answer would be, "No, they do not." However and fortunately, intelligent Christians, Jews, and people of conscience are becoming more empathetic to the Palestinian perspective. And it is their opinions and actions—as well as ours—that will change the world's paradigms.

Three

ACCURATE HISTORY OF ISLAM:
DISPELLING MYTHS

*"The farther backward you can look
the farther forward you will see."*

—WINSTON CHURCHILL

For those who are reading this book and have little or no knowledge about Islam, Islam means "submission to God" and is from the root word meaning "peace." Although, man gave the terms "Christianity" and "Judaism" to their religious ideology, Islam (submission to one God) was the name given by God. The Holy book that Muslims read is the Quran, which literally means "the recitation." (This definition means that God is directing humanity to read this Holy book.) The Quran states that God sent his book through the angel Gabriel (who is termed "the Holy Spirit") to Prophet Mohammed and is a guide to lead mankind into the light and out of darkness.

In the year 610 A.D., Prophet Mohammed brought an essential message to the Arabian Peninsula. He called for vast social reforms by implementing justice for the poor and oppressed. According to author Reza Aslan, Mohammed's message was new and different from other religions of its time and location. Aslan states that Mohammed's message was a "revolutionary one" of "moral accountability and social egalitarianism."[18] But was it? If we reflect, we can question whether "Mohammed's message" differentiated Islam from other religions of his time. Did the teachings of Islam call for a set of actions that differed from other monotheistic religions? And we can dispel myths put forth by modern propaganda against Islam.

Throughout history, no individual of any religion wanted to be oppressed. However, at times, when people of a particular religion gained power, they sometimes abused their power to oppress others who were not "the same religion," labeling them as "the other." This can be seen with the Christian Crusades into the Middle East, the colonization of Third World countries by Europeans, and right wing militant Zionists who have taken Palestinian territory, settled it, and have oppressed Palestinians in the occupied territories. Media sources, other than top tier media, inform us about the treatment of "the other" exemplified by the open-air prisons in Gaza.

Completely contradictory to how right wing militant Zionists act is the other end of the spectrum described within the historical tenets of the Islamic religion and also in some sects of the Orthodox Jewish religion. Islam calls on its believers to help the oppressed, whoever they are, regardless of religion, race, or economic status. Some Orthodox Jewish sects believe the same.

By analyzing prayer in the Muslim religion, we see that the first and most important prayer begins with "In the name of God, the Beneficent, the Merciful." According to the Merriam-Webster Dictionary, "Beneficent" means, "doing or producing good, an act of goodness, kindness and charity."[19]

Merciful means "forbearance from inflicting harm, compassionate treatment of others, disposition to exercise compassion or forgiveness, willingness to spare or help, or compassionate treatment of the unfortunate." "Mercy implies "compassion so encompassing that it enables one to forego punishing, even when justice demands it."[20] Thus, the most important Islamic prayer opens with verses describing God's mercy.

Another historical tenet in Islam involves charity. Charity does not exclusively mean making financial donations; it also includes acts of compassion, understanding, kindness, and tolerance. All of the synonyms of mercy, kindness, and charity mean that God can and will forgive everything of a repentant person. One of the sayings of Prophet Mohammed is, "The essence of religion is love." In fact, one characteristic of God is "The Loving".

If we reflect, we can ask ourselves if Muslims are fully following the mindset, spirit, and actions of Prophet Mohammed. His actions can be interpreted as a call to become proactive and inclusive of our Christian and Jewish brothers and sisters. If all Muslims strive to be proactive and assertive and reach out to the broader community—as thousands of Muslims did in Oslo, Norway, forming a ring of safety around the city's Jewish synagogue—then the millions of dollars spent on negative propaganda each year in the U.S. alone would probably have no bearing on the thoughts of the larger society.

Society would see the positive actions of Muslims and would become aware of their contributions as important and contributing role models. Because Muslims have little or no voice, many in the American public feel fear and prejudice. They have no facts on which to base their opinions except for inaccuracies and bias presented in top tier media.

Ironically, while Islam embraces their Christian and Jewish brothers, the right wing militant Zionists are murdering innocent Palestinian children and civilians in Gaza. Zionist propaganda uses projection as a defense by accusing Muslims and Arabs of doing the precise activity they engage in, such as terrorism and using humans as shields. Thousands of people in the West Bank, along with thousands in many countries throughout the world, are demonstrating to show support for their Palestinian brothers and sisters in Gaza.

The caution I convey is that, today, right wing militant Zionists are slaughtering Gazans; tomorrow, they might be senselessly murdering people on the West Bank; and next week, who knows where the militant Zionists or their soldiers will strike.

We do know the Israeli government seeks to demolish the ancient Palestinian village of Sasilia and remove all the residents. The Israeli government has asked the High Court to rule in its favor.[21] Therefore, it is unmistakable that the present Israeli government and their supporters want Palestinian land and will go to great lengths to confiscate it.

Evidently, those who support the occupation of Palestine will build a case, no matter how absurd, for public consumption. They think that most people are so naïve or ignorant of the facts that by repeating unfounded propaganda, over and over, they can further their goal. But, by looking at some of the historical facts about Islam, its roots, and its core beliefs, we can dispel the myths of modern propagandists.

A. Did Prophet Mohammed state he brought a new religion?

The Quran never stated that Prophet Mohammed brought a "new religion". In fact, the Quran states that Adam was the first Muslim and that Mohammed delivered the message of Islam in order to complete the religion. This indicates that other monotheistic religions of the time lacked some important information or needed additional information to alter or rectify some important concepts and actions. Prophet Mohammed espoused the Islamic viewpoint on monotheism and unity. He conceptualized Islam as a large umbrella that comprised all the major monotheistic religions within it. Therefore, Islam calls all monotheistic believers to submit to *one* God, the God of *all* religions and to do good works that all religions profess to want to perform.

The Quran, our Holy Book, speaks about Christians and Jews as "people of the book". As Prophet Mohammed preached, the Judaic Torah, the Christian Gospels, and the Islamic Quran, must be read as a single cohesive narrative about humanity's relationship to God.[22] Prophet Mohammed, himself, never said he brought a new religion.

In fact, in the Quran, when the Pharaoh (during Prophet Moses' time), was drowning, he said to God, "I become a Muslim, one who submits to God." Thus, Islam or submission to God was the message all the prophets brought to the world. All the prophets from Adam, Noah, Abraham and their descendants throughout history preached Islam, the religion of submitting to one God and performing good actions. According to the Quran, God told Prophet Mohammed to follow the beliefs of the Prophet Abraham, which is "belief in the one true God."

Further, the Quran never stated that it nullified previous original scriptures. The Quran states it is sent "as a confirmation of revelations that went before it and a fuller explanation."[23] According to Mohammed, Christians and Jews worshipped the same God, read the same scriptures and shared the same moral values as the Muslim community. Therefore, Mohammed believed these three religious groups comprised one major community. Consequently, he was favorable toward intermarriage between the three religions. In fact, he married a Jewish woman and a Christian woman after his beloved Khadija died. He asked his Muslim followers to join him in fasting on Yom Kippur. He never expected the Jews to convert to Islam as some authors incorrectly stated. Instead, he spoke of universal brotherhood and fellowship.

The Ten Commandments in Judaism are the same exact commandments in Islam. In fact about 23 commandments in Judaism are similar to Islamic commandments. A Jewish person is supposed to care about the oppressed which is the same as Islamic beliefs.

With regard to Christianity, Mohammed credited the Christian King of Ethiopia with saving the persecuted Muslims from the pagans. These pagans followed the Muslims all the way from Saudi Arabia to Ethiopia to ensure their persecution and murder because they infringed on the pagans' economic status quo. Later in Prophet Mohammed's life, he wrote a letter to Christians guaranteeing them, Muslim protection. This letter is on exhibit at a Turkish museum. Following in the footsteps of the Prophet, Imam Ali, a philosopher, author, warrior and the first male to accept Islam after the Prophet stated, "He who hurts Christians, hurts me."

B. Who is "Allah"?

"Allah" is the Arabic word for "God." In top tier media, in the U.S., "Allah" is presented in a disparaging or belittling way that diminishes the word. In fact, it said in such a way as to imply that Allah is an idol that Muslims worship. "Allah" is the Arabic word for "God." Therefore, many Christians in the Middle East as well as Muslims refer to God as "Allah" when they speak Arabic. Also, if church services in the Middle East are not held in Latin or Greek, the Arabic word "Allah" is used. Using the term, "Allah" in a degrading way within the English language is another technique to make Islam look like a foreign and non-monotheistic religion. Further, a religion is monotheistic if that religion believes in "one" God and "only one" God, which explains the concept of God in Islam.

C. Was Islam spread by the sword?

"If you are not careful, the newspapers
will have you hating the people who are
being oppressed and loving the people
who are doing the oppressing."

MALCOLM X

This is a profound statement. There are many myths perpetuated by top tier media to preserve the credibility of the Israeli occupation. One myth says that Muslims spread the message of Islam by the sword. The motive for this statement is obviously to imply that Islamic beliefs are not worthy on their own to attract converts and must rely on the threat of violence.

Islam, the fastest growing religion in the United States and the world, is *not* growing because of violence. In fact, most people of any religion, in contemporary society are repelled by violence. This fact alone disproves the "spread by the sword" propaganda message. If Islam were a violent religion, the number of Muslims would be decreasing, not increasing.

The Islamic edict of nonviolence is supported by Islamic scripture. Al-Ahzab, the translator of one edition of the Quran, explains in the commentary, Chapter 33: "The Holy Prophet never in his life took any initiative in waging any war and never committed or permitted any unprovoked aggression."[24] Excessive aggression was not permitted, and warfare was carried out under the strictest circumstances with the aim of establishing peace and justice through the religion of Islam.[25] In fact, Prophet Mohammed gave amnesty to everyone when he overtook Mecca, Saudi Arabia.

The stereotype that Islam is a warrior religion or spread by the sword was propaganda dating from the Crusades. At that time, in history, European Christians sent their soldiers to the Middle East to defeat the Muslims and acquire their territory. In contrast, according to author Reza Aslan, especially in the Near East where religions sanctioned state and territorial expansion, such expansion was indistinguishable from spreading one's own religious message. Thus, he said, every religion was a "religion of the sword."[26]

D. Has Muslim-Jewish conflict been occurring for hundreds of years?

The Islamic holy book states that "there is no compulsion in religion" and describes Jews and Christians as *ahlul kitaab*, or "people of the book." Consequently, under Islamic law, the rights of Jews and Christians were and are protected by Muslims; this includes protection against any form of forced conversion.[27]

Twice, the Romans expelled the Jews from Palestine and burned their buildings and temples. Salahedeen, a brave and famous Muslim ruler and commander during the Crusades, fought Richard the Lionheart in order to allow the Jews to return to Palestine. He was admired and very much esteemed for his courage and for respecting people of other religions. When facing Richard the Lionheart in battle, Richard was thrown off his horse. Rather than seizing the opportunity for victory, Salahedeen provided Richard with a new horse. Later, Richard became ill and was near death from a high fever. Salahedeen sent his own doctors to care for him[28] and bring food and cold water from nearby mountains to reduce Richard's fever.[29] Salahedeen's eventual victory over the Crusaders was instrumental in fostering the Jewish return to Palestine.

Further, in Andalusia, the Muslim-administered and governed part of Spain, Jews and Christians were treated with respect, granted civil rights, and allowed to practice their respective religions as long as they paid a special tax to the state. The special tax paid for upkeep of Islamic armies because the

Jews and Christians were not required to serve in the army. This was known as the Golden Age of Judaism which was under the leadership of Muslims who ruled for 500 years.

Historian Richard Bulliet used genealogies in medieval Islamic biographical dictionaries to estimate the percentage of the Spanish population that converted to Islam. He found an increase in conversions from 8 to 70 percent between the ninth and eleventh centuries.[30] While the precision of these numbers may be a question for scholarly debate, it is unquestioned that the Muslim population in Spain grew substantially during the Muslim caliphate.[31]

Finally, when Catholic monarchs Ferdinand and Isabella came to power in 1492 A.D., they expelled the Jews from Spain. Jewish people moved through southern Italy but were unwelcome. At that time, the Ottoman territories, including Turkey, were ruled by Islamic Sultan Abdul Hamid II. He welcomed the Jewish refugees and was happy to have them in the Ottoman territories due to their expertise as artisans.[32] Jews also fled to Morocco to be in the sanctuary of Muslim protection.

In more recent times, during the Holocaust, many Muslims aided the Jewish community. One courageous Muslim woman, Noor Inayat Khan, stood up to the Nazis to save the Jews. She was of Indian origin, living in Paris, and an enemy of the German Reich.

Noor Inayat Khan's mother was American and her father was an Indian Sufi. She was a brilliant girl who wrote children's books and was raised at the Sufi center, her parents' home in Paris. She learned the highest values and integrity from her father who attracted many followers to their home. As a young woman, she became a British agent during the war. When she was caught by the Nazis, she never lied and refused to give any information about the Allies. She escaped from prison but was quickly apprehended. Then the Nazis put her in solitary confinement surrounded by filthy conditions. When they still couldn't break her, they murdered her. The movie, *Enemy of the Reich: The Noor Inayat Khan Story* was produced about her determination and her endless strength to assist the Jewish community.[33]

This is just one of many stories of Muslims who helped Jews survive domination and extermination by the Nazis. Therefore, the myth that Muslims and Jews were hostile toward each other over hundreds of years is totally incorrect.

What is the reason that Islamic history has been intentionally falsified? First, clearly, the perpetrators believe that creating a myth of perpetual conflict between Jews and Muslims will serve as a rationalization for the right wing militant Zionists to occupy Palestinian land, diminish indigenous Palestinian rights, and oppress the people who live there. Second, the "perpetual conflict myth" is also used as a rationalization for the broader non-Muslim community to say, "There has been conflict between Muslims and Jews for hundreds of years and nothing has worked in the past. So why bother trying to do something to change the situation now? It is hopeless." Of course, this rationalization is a ploy to maintain the unfair, unjust status quo, and it is untrue. If people on both sides are open to positive change then change will occur.

E. Are any groups - the chosen ones?

Many times, we have heard that Jews are the "chosen ones" or "God's chosen people." What does that mean? Let us objectively look and reflect on the events that occurred at the time of the prophets.

First, when Noah's family was saved from the malicious unbelievers on Earth because they were drowned, there is no question that Noah and his family were chosen to survive the Great Flood. Later in history, Abraham (father of Judaism, Christianity and Islam) believed in One God. His small group of followers was definitely chosen above the idolaters. When Abraham asked if God would continue the covenant with his progeny, God told him that not all his progeny would be under the covenant. God would continue the covenant only with those who would keep the covenant with God.

Later, when Moses' people were in servitude and oppressed in Egypt, the Jewish people were definitely preferred or chosen over Pharaoh and his worshippers. In fact, God made a covenant with the people of Moses who led his people to safety by means of the exodus from Egypt. He intended to leave his people for 30 days in order to commune with God on Mount Sinai. However, when Moses stayed on the mountain for an additional ten days, Israel (the people of Jacob) created a golden calf (a symbol of materialism) and worshipped it, instead of worshipping God who saved them from slavery. This was the point in time when Israel did not keep their covenant with God, thus fulfilling God's prophesy to Abraham centuries earlier. Because the Jewish people broke the covenant, they were made to wander in the desert for 40 years.

After Moses, Jesus, son of Virgin Mary, was born with the spirit (power) of God. He taught people love and compassion. His followers became "chosen" over anyone who did not accept this message or maintain their covenant with God.

Lastly, Prophet Mohammed proclaimed, "One God and only One God; One who does not beget nor has He begotten," and announced social justice for the poor as well as the rich. At this point Muslims and others who believed in one God and did good deeds were also "chosen" to disperse God's clear message. Actually, according to the Quran, God formed a covenant with Abraham, Moses, and Mohammed.

In fact, the Quran states that God chose "Islam" for us. What does that mean? The religion of Islam, as previously stated, means submission to God, belief in one God, and performing good deeds; this is our guidance. This is different than the Jewish belief of one people being *chosen by God.* Thus, the message from God is that each person is responsible for his or her beliefs and actions, regardless of the stated religion.

Even Pope Francis I, who according to the Catholic precepts is the papal "descendent" of Jesus Christ, rejected the concept of "chosen people."[34] In a morning mass in St. Martha's House in October, 2014, the Pope said, "Those who feel they are the 'chosen ones' show a reluctance to be saved. It is the ruling class that closes the doors to the way in which God wants to save us. They say, 'We want to make the rules for our own salvation!'"[35]

Anne Marie Ameri, Ph.D.

F. Analysis of the Evolution of Humanity's View of God

Reflecting on God's actions in the early days of paganism versus belief in one God during the times of Noah, Abraham, and even Moses, we see how humanity views God. As we reflect further and consider how people view God today, we see an evolution in thought and God-consciousness.

This evolution begins with the early viewpoint that God was vengeful, and fiercely protective of his previously so called "chosen people", or "family of believers." Later, the idea of a compassionate God came into view. Now, the more modern opinion predominates; God is forgiving and loving. Along with this evolutionary shift is the notion in the old and new testaments that God, at the time of the prophets, was an abstract father figure who lived in Heaven. Today, people identify God as a divine entity who is close to us and whose spirit is *within* each individual. In actuality, the Quranic concept explains God as both abstract and close; that God's spirit (mercy) is *within* each of us. The Quran stated these concepts in the 6th century A.D., yet, people are just beginning to realize and understand this concept.

For those who accept the evolution of God as fierce protector, perhaps we can comprehend this view more fully if we reflect on the role of parents within familial society. As a mother or father, we would be vehemently protective of our children and this might be especially true if we had only one child. If anyone tried to hurt our only child, we might do anything and everything to protect our precious offspring. Under extreme provocation and danger to our offspring, one might become so angry that one would consider hurting or even consider killing the aggressor(s). In fact, this is exactly what God did during the times of Noah (to protect the innocent believers from the harmful actions of the pagans) and during the time of Moses when God cast plagues and pestilence upon the Egyptians (idolaters) in order to protect the Israelites (believers). This is the image of a wrathful God of ancient times. However, at the beginning of the Christian era through the teachings of Jesus, people began to see God as a divine entity exhibiting compassion and forgiveness to non-believers.

By the time of Prophet Mohammed nearly 600 years later, God, in the Quran, stated, "There is no compulsion (pressure, force or obligation) in religion." Thus, God said, each individual has the freedom to choose his or her actions and is responsible for the consequences of those actions. In other words, instead of God causing mass drowning's, earthquakes, or plagues to eradicate tyranny and destructive behavior, the Islamic holy book proclaims that each person either helps or hurts his *own soul* by his or her choices. Therefore, instead of God protecting humanity from itself, one needs to take personal responsibility for his or her own actions. This is one of the new perspectives that Mohammed brought to the world, the message that fulfilled or completed the previously established Jewish and Christian traditions.

If we attempt to understand our perception of God's behavior—or humans evolutionary views of God's behavior—we see that, according to the Jewish scriptures of the Old Testament, God was perceived as uncompassionate and even vengeful. This was welcomed by the Jews at that time because they viewed God as protective and so powerful that He quickly and easily administered severe punishment to their enemies, which included the pagans, the sinful, and the enslaving Egyptian idolaters.

Prophet Jesus and his followers believed that God looked upon their people as well as others with peace, compassion, and forgiveness. Perhaps this belief occurred because the community of believers in one God was more widespread, at that time, and, therefore, the community was not under threat of tyranny that could lead to nonexistence. On the other hand, perhaps, this belief came to correct a narrow-sighted viewpoint in thinking about God.

The teachings of the Prophet Mohammed also professed that God is compassionate, peaceful, forgiving, and also possesses the qualities of mercy and beneficence. Through Mohammed's proclamation of "no compulsion in faith," Jews and Christians were perceived as part of the broader community of believers with the dictum for all to know and respect each other, not to inflict hurt, vilify, or cause pain to the other. As such, Islam is seen as a "Universal Religion" with humanity perceived as one family where Adam and Eve are the parents of all.

God, perceived today by Islam and people who accept the concept of "one God of all humanity," believe that each person chooses his or her path—and has the right and responsibility to do so. With this belief, the myth of the "chosen ones" is neither necessary nor applicable. This occurred because humanity has changed their perception of God to a forgiving and loving God.

On the other hand, considering a different perspective, did we historically have a myopic view of God and God's actions? Did we misinterpret God's actions? Scholars may have selected certain major events on which to focus—earthquakes, floods, raining stones—but overlooked the mercy and compassion that God was providing humanity, throughout these periods. God has many characteristics and perhaps scholars have overlooked the love and compassion God expressed throughout history to *all* his believers: Muslims, Christians, and Jews as well as those of other faiths that are not as widely practiced. Wouldn't this also negate the "chosen one" theory?

The message in this evolution of thinking, for us today is simply this: In ancient times, God protected his small family of believers from malicious pagans or idolaters. Consequently, the interpretation, "God's chosen people," evolved. Perhaps that was the message the people of that time, with their yet to evolve thinking, needed to hear. Evidently, it worked for the religious groups at that time, but that philosophy no longer works today. If their conclusions were accurate, God would choose one set of "believers" over another. Historically, God chooses believers over idolaters. However, in contemporary society, we are *all* believers in God.

Unfortunately, some individuals and groups continue to feel entitled and consider themselves better than all "others" who they contend God has not "chosen". In truth, according to contemporary thinking, it is imperative that everyone—*all* of God's creation— perform to their potential. That is why self-hatred is so self-limiting and is not to be used as an excuse for anyone, Muslims included, to not to fulfill their potential.

Four

Basic Concepts and Tenets of Islam

The Quran explains two concepts that are of major significance. First, belief in *One* God, translates to *not* worship materialism, idols, or even oneself. Second, is to perform good deeds. This means a person is required to help others, care for his/her own needs, show respect to yourself and others, pray to God, and be charitable, both openly and secretly.

Please remember, the Quran states that God "guides you in Islam." The guidance through the Quran gives explanations, direction, mercy, and hopeful news for those who submit to God. Through this belief, God guides people of faith to believe in one God and to do good deeds—regardless of their chosen religion: Islam, Christianity, Judaism, or others. Anyone who has belief and good action is assured of being rewarded in the afterlife or heaven. Heaven in Islam is explained as a beautiful place where souls enjoy nearness in the presence of the Lord.

Another tenet of Islam tells its believers to respect and abide by the laws of each respective country. This is one reason that Islam blends in harmony within any country where it is practiced. The followers basically become part of the country's fabric and most make positive contributions to their nation. Islam is a peaceful, non-violent, and universal religion embracing all races, nationalities, and social statuses, and easily adapts to each country's cultural traditions, unlike the anti-Islamic rhetoric one hears.

A. Social Message of Islam
The social message in Islam is social justice with inalienable rights for *all* humanity. Among these rights are freedom from hunger and thirst, freedom to be sheltered, and freedom to practice one's chosen religion, whatever that religion happens to be. Because Islam means "submission to God," it states that humanity is one. There is no superiority based on race, nationality, gender, or status, which are manmade designations designed to discriminate against individuals and divide humanity according to physical or social distinctions.

B. Principles of Justice in Islam
From the Old Testament onward, God selected his prophets. In some cases, the prophets were able to select their companions,

as Moses did with his brother Aaron, with the approval of God. In other cases, the companion selected the prophet's religion as much as the prophet selected his companion, as in the case of Prophet Mohammed and his young cousin, Ali.

Ali was a great thinker, philosopher, leader, and warrior. In fact, Ali embraced Islam when he was between 12- 14 years old. The Prophet asked Ali to please go home and ask his father's permission to become a Muslim. However Ali said, "No, I will make the decision." All of Ali's (Imam Ali's) characteristics led Prophet Mohammed to believe that he wished for Ali to take over leadership of the Muslims after his death. During a stop at Al Ghadir, Prophet Mohammed verbalized his intentions. Ali proved to be more than capable of such an assignment, living by core Islamic principles; by not discriminating against others, but by helping the homeless, providing for the less fortunate of all religions, aiding the oppressed and practicing his beliefs of justice and compassion.

On one occasion, when thieves burst into a gathering and ripped jewelry off of the women in attendance, none of the men did anything. Rather, they silently stood and watched the robbers grab the jewelry and leave. Ali admonished them saying, "You seem to look like men but you are not men. I feel ashamed to know you. If you were to die [at the hands of the robbers], then you would die, but at least you would have been helping the oppressed." Imam Ali died as he lived, with a strong faith in God and Islamic principles. He is called "Imam" which means "leader".

After Prophet Mohammed died, there was a political power struggle that caused a rift between another leader, Abu Bakr and Imam Ali over leadership of the Islamic Empire. Aggressors injured Fatima (Imam Ali's wife, the Prophet Mohammed's daughter) and the injury shortened her life. But even with such provocation, Ali remained patient, peaceful, and nonviolent for the sake of unity in Islam. He was a strong, resilient, reflective and compassionate man.

The story of Ali's death illustrates his adherence to the Islamic principle of justice. Ali was killed by one stroke to the neck by a poisonous sword. The man hired to kill him knew Ali and worked for him many years before the incident. Ali did not die immediately. Ali had this man brought to him while on his deathbed and asked, "Did I not treat you well?" The man said, "Yes, you treated me well." Ali asked him what happened to make him want to kill him. The man said that he was promised wealth and freedom by an idolater if he killed Ali. He said that, for 40 days, he dipped the sword into poison, thus indicating that his action was, indeed, premeditated.

The significance this story is that, at this time in Islamic history, if an idolater or an idolater's hired person, intentionally killed a believer, that idolater could also be killed. This form of capital punishment was amplified if a major leader was murdered; in that case, the leader's community would declare war on the entire tribe of the man who was the murderer.

But Ali also knew, from his connection with Prophet Mohammed and his study of the Quran, that it is "better to forgive." Therefore, Ali directed that his followers employ a milder form of justice that embodied both the law of the land

and the forgiveness tenet of the Quran. He told his men to *only kill this man*, the murderer. He also told his followers to use the same exact sword that the murderer used and to strike the man with a single blow to his neck, just as the murderer had done to kill Ali. Ali was firm in his resolve that his followers were not to use Ali's murder as an excuse to kill more than this man.

Ali stated, "The success of a society is judged by how they treat their fellow man." A society whose people are oppressed is not a successful society, nor is a society that seeks unlawful revenge.

Today, the Israeli government continues to oppress the poor in Gaza and the West Bank. The Israeli government and top tier media in both that country and the United States rationalize the Israeli government's aggressive and brutal actions. Yet, if we are to reflect on Islamic justice, according to Ali's standard, neither Israel nor the U.S. would be deemed a successful society.

Many times people in the U.S., Israel, and elsewhere are discriminated against because of their skin color, country of origin, social status, or religion. The Quran tells humanity that people are not to be judged on these characteristics but rather on their character and good deeds. According to the tenets of the Quran, the Torah, and the Bible, if we treat our neighbors and fellow citizens as we wish to be treated, then violence and hypocrisy would be eliminated. Consequently, our societies—and all the world's societies—would become more successful.

Section II

BENEFITS FOR THE POWERFUL WHEN
MANIPULATING MUSLIM YOUTH

Five

PSYCHOLOGICAL AND
PHYSIOLOGICAL WARFARE

Declassified CIA document NND 877092 defines psychological warfare as a military tactic "to undermine the enemy's will and capacity to resist."[36] The document also states
that the "aim is more successfully treated if broken down into
two subsidiary aims, namely, demoralization and encourage-
ment or persuasion."[37]

These strategies are, in essence, forms of warfare and a process called "mirroring," in which an individual or member of
Group A actually fears what he or she accuses Group B of doing, such as acts of "terrorism". Through the use of mirroring,
Group A intends to make Group B become inactive, paralyzed,
and subsequently, do nothing even though they are abused and
provoked by Group A. When this happens, members of abused

Group B will begin to lose respect for themselves. Once Group B becomes demoralized and its resistance is low, Group A has won the battle.

Research has been performed regarding the results of psychological warfare when combined with physical abuse, particularly among Palestinian children whose families have been subjected to Israeli aggression and abuse. Upon seeing or learning of atrocities to their family members, children suffer severe psychological trauma. They lose hope and joy in living and in life itself. Under the Israeli occupation, research findings show these children are suffering immensely, are treated like adults, and endure the harshest of conditions.[38]

Documentation by the United Nations Committee on the Rights of the Child shows that high rates of Palestinian children are being held in solitary confinement inside Israel. Some are blindfolded, some have restraints used on them, and some are tortured.[39] Some Palestinian children are forced to sign confessions that are written in Hebrew, which is the language of Israelis and obviously not understood by these children. Palestinians communicate in the Arabic language.[40] Furthermore, there is great concern over the Israeli practice of arresting (abducting) Palestinian children at night and placing them in solitary confinement.[41] The Israeli military know that children are defenseless and can be easily traumatized under such harsh conditions. This appears to be a strategy to break the spirit of the children, and demoralize them, leaving a psychological wound that will follow them into adulthood.

Research has also been performed in the United States to measure the physiological responses of African, Asian, and Latin American youth who live under the influence of U.S. culture and may feel the effects of discrimination. Lisa Kiang, Associate Professor of Psychology and Terry Blumenthal, Professor of Psychology at Wake Forest University conducted experiments to connect social and emotional experiences of discrimination to physical responses as a measure of a person's resilience to discrimination. They studied college students from ethnically diverse backgrounds measuring startle eye blink reactions, which serve as an indicator of basic neurological functioning to overt racial rejection, subtle racial rejection, and racial acceptance images.

They used this sensitive measure to find which participants were sensitive to racial rejection. They found that participants who were highly sensitive to racial rejection and those who believed that persons of other ethnicities or nationalities did not value their group were more negatively biased by the images they saw. "If individuals have a hard time processing acceptance, all they have left is rejection," explained Kiang, who believes this research is a step toward better understanding the social experiences of racism.[42]

How did these individuals of marginalized groups become so sensitized to racial rejection? How will their lives be affected by the rejection they feel and their negative bias of filtering out acceptance images? Looking at these research studies, it is apparent that youth are affected negatively, by these adverse influences. Youth who are affected may need parental, adult and even psychological assistance to become better able to cope with the psychological trauma experienced by them.

Children and youth are the most vulnerable within any society, regardless of religion, ethnicity or country. If the goal of right wing Zionists is to break the spirit of the Arab and Muslim children, then our Muslim communities must put structures in place to help our youth feel strong enough to resist this psychological oppression.

It is important to recognize that strategies to negate the power of minorities, and especially their youth, are not new. The strategies are used to neutralize, reduce, or eliminate any influence that a politically unrepresented or weak community may generate. For example Huma Abedin, (former aide to Hillary Clinton, former Secretary of State and U.S. Presidential candidate, hopeful, for the Democratic Party in 2016), was accused by Michelle Bachmann and others of being a front for the Muslim Brotherhood.[43] It is easy to see through these accusations such as those leveled against Abedin by organizations and people who are pro-occupation of Palestine and don't want Muslims in positions of power or influence within the United States. In other words, those supporting this political agenda are engaging in "psychological warfare." Apparently, the militant Zionists want all the power in their own hands; hence the story about her being a front for the Muslim Brotherhood.

These accusations were so ludicrous and baseless that even conservative Republican Senator John McCain came to her defense; he said, "Abedin has a commitment to American ideals."[44] One month later, President Obama also defended Abedin, calling her "an American Patriot."[45]

As a consequence of the aforementioned injustices, Muslim adults and leaders must create a mental set of resilience and defiance for our youth. Our leaders must understand that impressionable youth, as well as adults, are affected by propaganda, "hate speech" tactics, and media assaults that are designed to reduce or eliminate our political power. Isn't this part of "colonialism," pursuing expansionism, maintaining power, control and finances? When a group attempts to "break" your will, it is the adults' responsibility to teach our youth coping skills such as resilience and a defiant attitude in the face of injustice.

Six

How Our Youth Are Affected

During the impressionable years of youth, it is normal for young people to be frustrated, angry, or disappointed because their idealistic views differ greatly from reality. Additionally, some Muslim youth may feel isolated because of the mounting pressure caused by the overwhelming negative misinformation they encounter about Islam.

Adolescents, in general, seek novelty and are sometimes risk takers. With their brains not fully mature, adolescents can benefit by slowing down, thinking things through, and reflecting about the consequences of their behavior. They could reduce their impulsivity and recklessness by reflecting and talking to the wise part of their mind before making decisions. They can also seek the advice of trusted adults. Thus, they can "thrive" instead of accepting or "settling for" less than what they deserve.

Traditional Muslim and Arabic names and identities have been given a negative connotation in the U.S. by mainstream top tier media. As a result many Muslim parents in the United States worry that they or their children will be denied access to equal opportunities unless they take every possible step to "assimilate" into American culture. Therefore, it is becoming more and more common to see Arab-Americans—as many as 37 percent in the U.S.—take on Western-sounding, Anglicized names. For example, "Mohamed" is often changed to "Mo" or "Mike" in an effort to better fit in

Discrimination is not a one-sided problem; rather, it is a problem that involves both the discriminator and the discriminated. Yes, some people are prejudiced, but some of our youth also accept and internalize these prejudices and try to change their identities to avoid being discriminated against.

Because these youths come from diverse backgrounds with different cultural ideals and values, they may also feel as though they fit in on one level of society, but still do not feel totally accepted as fully "American." Perhaps mainstream "America" is not fully accepting of "marginalized groups." Many youth feel as if they are in limbo; they belong neither to one culture nor the other. This state of limbo further contributes to feelings of insecurity, which perpetuates prejudice and a further loss of self-esteem. These feelings of marginalization put our youth at risk because they may, at times, think illogically, impulsively, or without objectivity.

As mentioned previously, an oft-repeated narrative in the conservative media, in particular, is that Arabs or Muslims are associated with terrorism. Because many of our youth, may have allowed the media to define them, they may feel a need to prove they are the opposite of what the media portrays. Some youth may wither in the background from their insecurities. Some may have a fear of failure resulting from consistent media assaults that prevent these youth from realizing their full potential. Frustrated and angry, some may choose unproductive outlets, turning to illegal activities. Others may drop out of college, saying they just want to have fun, not thinking or making any long-term plans for their life. In each of these cases, the youth who choose such diminutive and self-destructive actions are regrettably short-changing themselves instead of making the most of their human potential.

If you reflect, you will understand that media accusations against Islam have nothing whatsoever to do with religion. Associating terrorism with Islam would be the same as blaming all Jews for the conflict in Palestine. Politicians and media are fully aware that the powers that control the media also influence peoples' minds.

The media uses the "Muslim" as "terrorist" tactic because it is a simple attention-grabbing sound bite that creates a fearful visualization in citizens' imagination. To clarify, this generalization can be interpreted as right wing media saying, "We don't like your stance on Israel and Palestine, and we will do whatever we can to stifle the accurate expression of thoughts or positive actions to help Palestinians. We will do everything within our power to silence your ability to present your thoughts and ideas. We will prevent anyone from taking you seriously by discrediting you from being perceived as a well-respected member of society. Further, we will try our utmost to degrade you as a human being. Consequently, you will be afraid to speak up and defend yourself, let alone express your ideas or your cause."

Christopher Bail outlined the phenomenon of how anti-Muslim fringe groups became mainstream. A description of this book indicates that extremists belonging to hundreds of organizations are attempting to shape the discourse on Islam.[46]

Right wing militant Zionists will strategize about how to do all that is possible to make Muslims appear and feel like the "out group" minority who are not accepted by the "in group" majority. The Zionist media knows that if Muslims are not trusted, it will be much more difficult, if not impossible, for them to obtain any but the most menial jobs and, therefore, importantly, they will be significantly tarnished if they attempt to participate in the political process.

The same phenomenon occurs when the media generalizes and refers to Muslims as "Islamists" or "radical Islam" despite the fact that Islam is not radical. Does the media call Jews "Judaists" and "radical Jews" or Christians "Christianists", or "radical Christians", when the actions of a fraction of the people from these religious groups divert from mainstream social norms? The media does not vilify their religions.

When an individual who belongs to either the Christian or Jewish faith performs a violent act, the media never describes them on the basis of their religion. Often, their faith is not even disclosed. These people are not labeled "radical Christians" or "radical Jews." Nor do we hear the terms "Christian terrorists" or "Jewish terrorists" even though persons of those faiths have committed acts of terror, even against the United States.

In 1995, for example, Timothy McVeigh, who was raised Catholic, detonated a truck bomb in front of the Federal Building in Oklahoma City, Oklahoma,. The attack killed 168 people and injured over 600, and is, according to the U.S. government and was the most significant act of domestic terrorism in U.S. history at that time.[47] But how often did the media link him with his religion? With McVeigh, Internet bloggers loudly proclaimed: "McVeigh was not a Christian."[48]

If you ask the religion of a non-Muslim who committed a violent act, you may likely be informed that the person's religion has nothing to do with their actions as an individual. In fact, in a television interview, in 1995, after the Oklahoma bombing, anti-Islamic "terrorism expert," Steven Emerson, incorrectly suggested the bombings showed a "Middle Eastern trait." [49] He later said he "learned a lesson" from that experience.[50] Nevertheless, his organization continues to make inaccurate and incendiary statements about Muslims while maintaining its tax exempt status.

The violent individual of Christian or Jewish persuasion is either perceived as mentally ill or his behavior is rationalized by publicizing negative factors from his childhood. With this precedent in place for Christians and Jews, the question can be asked, "When the violent person happens to have ties to Islam, why is the religion vilified along with the individual?"

It appears obvious the media has two sets of rules—and it is imperative that Muslims, regardless of age, but especially our youth, recognize this. The effect of these media distortions with regard to Islam is, in itself, an act of verbal and psychological violence, terrorism, and discrimination toward Islam, Islamic holy sites, and Muslims in general.

What are Muslims doing about this ethnic intimidation? First, and most importantly, we must realize this media ploy is a treacherous strategic game plan imposed on unsuspecting Muslims and the broader non-Muslim majority in general. Second, Muslim parents especially, must educate and spread the word to our young people about the ways they are being marginalized. We must convey to our youth that the agenda of the predominantly Zionist controlled media is an attempt to discourage them—and we must then encourage them to not only recognize the negativity but to be resilient, positive in their thinking, and begin discourse with others. The youth need to understand not to hesitate for a second, but to be confident and focused about working toward their goal, and eventually they will achieve this goal.

We must remind our youth—and often ourselves—of the maxim: "If you repeat something enough, people will believe it." This is true of both negativity by top tier media and positivity within practitioners of our Islamic faith.

A. Naiveté Can Hurt You

"If you have a new friend who is speaking to you about 'violent jihad,' you should beware. This person may be an informant." This information is printed on the Muslim Legal Fund of America pamphlets and handouts to warn our community to be vigilant of surreptitious behavior by deceptive individuals.

How can we help our youth become aware of potentially dangerous situations in which they could become ensnared? In an investigative documentary produced by Al Jazeera's Investigative Unit in regard to tactics used by the FBI, Imam Fazaga, (leader of the mosque) from the Orange County Islamic Foundation, in Orange County, California, stated, "It literally boils down into, go and find terrorists. If you can't find terrorists within the Muslim community, create the terrorists."[51]

One FBI informant, Craig Monteilh, nicknamed, the "Body Builder" explained one FBI scheme to lure a Muslim informant. He said he "would take unsuspecting youth to the gyms because the youth get tired and would let their guard down at the gym."[52] According to Monteilh, the method the FBI used to entice a person to become an informant is summarized by the acronym MICE: "M is for money to bribe them, I is for ideology (in this case, religion), C is for compromise (find "compromising information" that makes a person vulnerable, such as criminal activity or drug arrests), and E is for ego." [53]

Our society is rich in wealth but, at times, is emotionally and intellectually impoverished. Let us look at the dynamics at play between the potentially alienated youth and the FBI informant.

When our youth are perceived as the "out group," they may feel psychologically alienated. Because they may feel isolated, they may become more susceptible to intense pressure partly as a result of the amount of negativity they hear about Islam. If a person then appears on the scene (the gym, the mosque, or youth hang-outs) and appears to befriend this youth, this "new friendly acquaintance" may be very persuasive. In fact, it may be difficult for an isolated person to say "no" to this new acquaintance because the unassuming and vulnerable youth values this new friendship.

At first, the "new friend" may just want to do things together. Then the "new friend" may begin to try to convince the youth that his or her ("the new friend's") opinion and logic is correct, more relevant, and more important than what the youth has been raised to believe. At this point, the "new friend" has become the dominant, superior one, and the Muslim youth has become the passive, inferior one. At this point, the "new friend" will suggest some illegal ideas and ask for input regarding how they might commit acts of violence together. Because of his training and employment with a clandestine agency, such as the FBI, the "new friend" will be very persuasive and will have access to materials and financial capital for these destructive acts that the youth otherwise would be incapable of obtaining.

Unfortunately, the Muslim youth doesn't know is that this so-called "new friend" is tape- recording the conversations. The "new friend" may, now, start talking about "jihad" and "how Muslims are treated throughout the world." The "new friend" likely will suggest that the Muslim youth, now won over through this ruse, commit the acts of violence. An even more efficient form of luring our unsuspecting youth is through social media or in the case of males, luring young men with sham girlfriends.

Fortunately, most of the time, youth who are approached by an informant in this manner resist or step away. Hopefully, they will talk to a responsible adult. This is when the Islamic community must step forward. Whether in response to such an incident—or better yet, before—we must remind our youth, as well as his or her friends: "Don't allow this or any other person to influence you to perform any violent acts. The person's persuasiveness is a ruse to fool you. He or she will be very convincing because his or her job depends on it and they have been trained in the art of deception." They have employed Arabic speakers and Muslims that they might use to deceive you.

One case in point occurred in Dearborn, Michigan, in March 2014. Mohammad Hassan Hamdan, a 22-year-old asthmatic with one functioning lung, was arrested by federal officials at Detroit Metropolitan Airport on his way to Lebanon after a "friend/informant" told the FBI that Hamdan wanted to travel to Syria to fight alongside Hezbollah. The ploy of this unsuspecting youth's "new friend," as described previously, actually happened to Hamdan; his account was described in an article by Tresa Baldas in *The Detroit Free Press* on March 17, 2014.[54]

Because it is essential for our Muslim youth to understand the previous facts and circumstances, I will speak directly to the youth here:

If you, as young Muslims, refuse to be enticed into committing illegal acts, these provocateurs will lose their jobs because, without convincing you to perform a violent act, their job is unnecessary. I intentionally repeat myself, because this is an important point to remember.

If you are foolish enough to follow a "new friend's" suggestion and direction, or say something violent on internet or elsewhere on social media or personally, even in jest, the law could easily brand you as a "terrorist" and you could be sentenced to life in prison. Your so-called wrongdoing will be quickly broadcast as another example that "Muslims are terrorists." That is unfair and untrue about Islam, your community, and yourself. You will lose your right to travel freely throughout this country and the world, to get a job, to have a girlfriend or boyfriend, to be married and have children, and to see your family and parents.

Therefore, it is imperative that you *learn to question* whenever you doubt a person or that person's ideas, especially if that idea is for *you* to commit an act of violence or an act contrary to your Islamic values. Be forewarned also that a person who approaches you may be one of your true friends who you have known for a long time. Maybe this person has previously been solicited and taken in by an informant and is now reaching out to you for either illicit collaboration or with a plea for help.

It is important to analyze the information you hear and see, whether with a "new friend" or a "trusted friend", either through social media or personally. Denying the possibility that you are being set up and saying, "No, it cannot be." or

"Why would someone want to set *me* or *us* up?" is unhelpful and prevents you from facing the reality and severity of the situation in which you—yes, *you*—are involved. One way to appraise whether you should engage in a behavior is to ask yourself if you would like to see yourself and this behavior reported in the headlines of your newspaper.

Let's talk more about the government using social media sites for "new friends" to possibly trick you. A seemingly "friendly" site can lure unsuspecting, vulnerable youth to join "radical groups." Of course, these "groups" may pretend to be associated with Islam but, instead, it is highly likely they could be established and monitored by governmental policing agencies.

So, youth, be very cautious about joining groups or posting any material, even in jest that could be used against you. Remember, anything you post will likely remain somewhere on the internet, and the government and others will likely see it, even years, later.

Parents need more effective support systems and more reporting mechanisms in the community to help those youth who are vulnerable. (Please see the Chapter on Recommendations.) Now, more than ever, it is important for the parents to ensure that our children follow the values they were raised with.

B. Only One Percent of "Terrorists" Caught by the FBI Are Really Terrorists[55]

Even though top tier media has created the falsehood that "Muslims are terrorists," nothing could be further from the truth. Trevor Aaronson, author of *The Terror Factory*, exposed the FBI's undercover sting operations for the farce they are.[56] Aaronson appeared on the AlterNet Radio Hour and was interviewed by Joshua Holland. Aaronson said of 500 defendants charged with federal crimes involving international terrorism, about 250 were charged with immigration violations or lying to the FBI and that was supposedly linked to terrorism; however, no charges involving a terrorist plot were ever filed against these 250 people. Then about 150 were caught in a sting operation that was solely the creation of the FBI through an informant or undercover agent who provided the opportunity (idea) and the means (weapons and devices) to carry out an act of terrorism. Only about three to five of the 500 arrested, (less than one per cent), were actually involved in some sort of plot that utilized weapons either created or acquired by the arrested persons or were connected to international terrorists in some way. Most of the other people caught were poor and unemployed, had mental problems, or were disenfranchised. As marginalized people, they were most vulnerable to FBI selection techniques. [57]

Undercover surveillance is the largest part of the FBI's annual budget. Is it necessary or even appropriate for Congress to spend $3 billion on these FBI's counter-terrorism programs each year? Apparently these manufactured sting operations are ways for the U.S. government to rationalize the need for Congress to continue financing the FBI's counter-terrorism activities. This motivates me to ask, "Was the Boston Marathon bombing one way to rationalize continuing the $3 billion budget?"

C. Boston Marathon Bombing

This section may challenge your perception that the media and the FBI present factual and accurate information. Let us examine the occurrence of the Boston Marathon Bombing and the evidence that contradicts the popular beliefs against the perpetrators of the bombing. If you use critical thinking skills, you may find yourself asking, "Is everything we were told true? Could the police, FBI, or media have fabricated some, much, or even all of the so-called 'facts' of the Boston Marathon bombing case?"

On April 15, 2013, the day of the Boston Marathon, a security consultant agency from Craft International Services or Blackwater was "coincidentally," carrying out a drill. All of the people in that firm were carrying black backpacks. Video footage confirmed that the two exploded bombs came from black backpacks.

Dzhokhar Tsarnaev, 19 years of age, was an unemployed student who was later convicted of planting a bomb at the 2013 Boston Marathon. At the time of the bombing, Dzhokhar was carrying a light gray backpack, which meant his backpack didn't match the color of the backpacks that exploded and killed three persons while injuring 264 others.[58] His older brother, Tamerlane Tsarnaev, age 26, presumably unemployed, was killed by police days after his role in the bombing. I say "presumably unemployed" because Dzhokhar's attorney presented evidence suggesting that Tamerlane had previously been approached by the FBI to become an informant.

An eyewitness at the Boston Marathon bombing, Ali Stevenson, a cross country coach from the University of Mobile and a runner in the marathon, said there were bomb-sniffing dogs at the beginning and end of the race and it was announced from loudspeakers, "This is just a drill. Don't be concerned."[59]

More than one source confirmed that Israeli police headed to the U.S. to help in the investigation immediately following the event.[60] About four days after the Boston bombing, law enforcement officers killed Tamerlane Tsarnaev after he was apprehended and stripped naked. There was a picture of him standing naked and handcuffed directly outside of a police car.[61] Fox News staff said the cause of death was bullet wounds and injuries from an explosion.[62] So how did the story become twisted, that he was killed in a shootout with police and run over by an automobile driven by his brother, Dzhokhar?

After an intense house-to-house search by the police, a homeowner found Dzhokhar, bloodied and injured, lying in a covered boat in the homeowner's backyard. Law enforcement officers shot 200 rounds at Dzhokhar, one which directly hit his vocal chords. Dzhokhar was taken to Beth Israel Deaconess Medical Center. Then, as soon as he could utter his first word, he was transferred to a prison hospital.

In court, evidence presented by the authorities, alleged that Dzhokhar, while hiding in the boat, bloodied and injured, wrote on the boat's interior the reason he and his brother perpetrated the bombing, which was because of the way Muslims are treated in Afghanistan.

A critical thinker would ask: What does the treatment of Muslims in Afghanistan have to do with people running the Boston Marathon in the United States? Also: Why would a person who is injured and hiding in a boat want to write the reason for committing the crime that could later be used against him as an admission of guilt? I believe this story was an attempt by authorities to portray Dzhokhar as a terrorist in order to be tried in a closed military court. Dzhokhar, however, was eventually tried in an open court in Boston, the city where the bombing occurred, and, not surprisingly, found guilty on all 30 counts.

As a follow up to the Boston Marathon bombing, the FBI claimed Dzokhar's friends were involved. Purportedly, Dzokhar sent texts to his friends and told them to take what they wanted from his apartment. Does that mean Dzokhar's friends participated in the crime? Does that lead to judging Dzokhar guilty of the murders of the Boston Marathon? Or is it merely, at best, circumstantial information?

News reported that Tamerlane and Dzokhar's mother said, "The FBI knew her sons." She also said that a young man with a red beard, presumably either an acquaintance or "friend" (emphasis on the word "friend") of one of her sons, came to her house and "opened their eyes about what was happening to Muslims" in Russia and other countries. Using critical thinking skills, might we not ask: Wasn't Dzokhar's mother, who was from a separatist part of Russia, already knowledgeable about how Muslims were treated in her homeland?

I ask: If an Imam's lecture at a mosque is inflammatory and leads someone in his congregation to commit acts of violence, wouldn't the government take him to court and seek conviction on terrorism charges? Likewise, why wasn't this man with the red beard charged since his words were inflammatory and presumably led to a terrorist act? Or even more fundamentally: Who was this person and what was his role in the Boston Marathon bombing? Why didn't we hear more about him? Was he an agent provocateur?

The defense attorneys who represented Dzokhar Tsarnaev said in a court filing that the FBI was attempting to recruit Tamerlane to be an FBI informant and to report on activities within the Chechen and Muslim communities in Boston. The same court filing stated the government denied this allegation and quoted a March 14, 2014, statement, "The government has no evidence that Tamerlane Tsarnaev was solicited by the government to be an informant."[63]

Some logical questions come to mind: Because the government does not need to provide evidence, is that sufficient reason to believe they did not try to solicit him as an informant? Was Tamerlane an informant? Were he and his brother being duped into carrying out a deceptive 'false flag' or sting operation?

If Tamerlane and Dzokhar thought they actually carried out the bombing, would they be so reckless and naive to stop to purchase a half gallon of milk immediately after the attack? Would they stay in the Boston area? What had the Chechen Muslim community ever done to cause harm in the United States? Why did the government want Tamerlane to inform on his community?

During the trial, the prosecution spoke about the sophisticated manner in which the bomb was made, leading them to wonder if others were involved. Additional evidence suggested that the prosecution flip-flopped on whether the black powder used in making the explosive was found in Tamerlane's apartment. So the question remains, "Who actually made the bomb and where was it made?"[64]

In another aspect of this story, the FBI also "visited" a young man, Ibrahim Todashev, who was supposedly a friend of Tamerlane because both previously worked out at the same gym near Boston. Todashev now lived in Orlando, Florida. He was married, although he and his wife, Rena Todashev, had been estranged for years, but remained on good terms. Todashev's mother in law, Elena Teyer, said when Rena and Todashev wanted to marry, she knew he was a good man and approved of him. After a period of time of estrangement from his wife, he began living with his girlfriend, Tatiana Gruzdeva.

Masha Gessen, in her book *The Brothers: The Road to an American Tragedy*, says this wasn't the first time the FBI had talked with Todashev. They interviewed him three times in their offices. They wanted his estranged wife and his girlfriend to spy on him. When both declined, the FBI caused immigration problems for them and detained his girlfriend in jail.[65] The FBI told Todashev this interview in his apartment would be the last.[66] Unfortunately, that was to become true.

A media report from *The Muslim Observer* newspaper said three agents who identified themselves as FBI from Boston entered Todashev's apartment in Orlando, Florida. A local FBI agent named Chris also entered the apartment but one of the FBI agents from Boston, asked him to leave shortly before the killing of Todashev was about to take place.[67]

The FBI started to "interview" Todashev at 7:30 pm. His friend, Khusen Taramov, was at Todashev's apartment when the FBI arrived but was told to leave. Worried about Todashev, Khusen waited in the parking lot. At 11:30 pm, an FBI agent told him to leave the parking lot and made sure he was away from the premises by riding with Khusen in Khusen's car to a restaurant. The agent then called for someone to come and pick him up from the restaurant to take him back to Todashev's apartment. Todashev was allegedly killed by FBI agent Aaron McFarlane at 12:15 am. Does this action make the killing look like it was premeditated?

Who is Aaron McFarlane, the alleged killer? He was a 41-year-old FBI special agent and a former police officer with the Oakland police department in California. During his four-year career as an Oakland police officer, according to *The Guardian*, "He was named with another officer in two lawsuits alleging brutality, faced four internal affairs investigations, was accused of falsifying reports and abruptly stopped cooperating as a witness in a trial against colleagues accused of beatings and false arrests."[68] When he left the department in 2004, he had a pension of $50,450 a year.[69] Then ten years later, the Boston FBI hired him. That is the man the FBI sent to interrogate Todashev.[70]

The spin on this story was the agents were "just minutes" away from Todashev signing a confession, saying he and Tamerlane performed a violent crime three years earlier. The media initially reported that the FBI killed Todashev because he had a weapon. Soon afterwards, the media changed the story stating that the FBI said Todashev had a long object not a gun. Then the story changed to "his body was a weapon" based on the fact that Todashev was involved in mixed martial arts and was previously a wrestler in Boston. Once again, the story changed, alleging that Todashev threw a coffee table at the agents and reached for a metal broom.

Witnesses stated there were four to six FBI agents who entered his small apartment. Two to three weeks later, National Public Radio (NPR) reported that Massachusetts police and Florida police also accompanied the FBI to Todashev's home.

The medical examiner allowed Elena Teyer to see Todashev's body. From a significant bruise and contusion over the cheekbone, she surmised that an FBI agent or another police officer "forcefully struck" Todashev on the left side of the head while he was still alive. The body also revealed that Todashev had been shot seven times in vital organs with the final shot *in* the *top of his head,* slightly toward the back of the head, a wound that seems to indicate that it was inflicted posthumously. His body was found just inside the front door of his apartment, with what may have been a final "parting shot" while exiting the room. [71]

Elena was reluctantly allowed to enter Todashev's apartment. She saw blood on the floor but none on the walls. (It is possible the walls could have been washed.) She thus believes that all the shots, including the final shot in the top of Todashev's head, were fired while Todashev was lying on the floor, [72] trying to escape by crawling away from the agents.[73] Alternatively, if the blood had been washed off the walls then evidence could have been tampered with.

The *Detroit Free Press* reported that a Florida prosecutor, in May 2014, cleared the FBI agent, McFarlane, who alledgedly shot and killed Todashev. In court, the FBI agent said he shot Todashev after he lunged at him with a lethal object.[74] At the time of the killing, however, Todashev was on crutches from knee surgery. What was the "lethal object?" Was it the metal broom mentioned in earlier media reports or might it have been one of his crutches?

You might ask yourself, was there ever an FBI agent who was found guilty of wrongful murder? According to a *New York Times* report, quoted by Dave Lindorff, in an article for the magazine Counterpunch, dated March 24, 2014, out of 150 agent shootings of witnesses or suspects over an 18-year span, all 150 agents were cleared.[75]

Documents showed that one of the agents in Todashev's apartment on that tragic night of the interview texted, "Who is your daddy?" when the agent thought Todashev was going to sign an admission that he and Tamerlane committed a violent crime three years previously, in Walton, Massachusetts.[76]

Ironically—and sadly—Todashev's estranged wife, Rena, said she has evidence from his credit cards that he was not even in Walton, Massachusetts, on the day the murders were committed.[77] So why was he "interviewed and killed?"

Did Todashev know information that the FBI did not want publicized? Lindorff's article in Counterpunch suggests that Todashev may have been considered a key character witness for the defense in the Boston Marathon bombing. Was that the reason he had to be eliminated?

And what about harassment of those closely associated with Todashev? His girlfriend, Tatiana Gruzdeva, was deported by the U.S. Immigration and Customs Enforcement Agency (ICE) at the FBI's urging even though she had a valid visa and no criminal history. His friend Khusen Taramov left the U.S. to attend a funeral and was barred from returning to the U.S. even though he had a valid Green Card. Therefore, all of the witnesses of the witnesses were deported, jailed, or not allowed to return into the U.S.[78] Todashev's mother-in-law, Elena Teyer, stated that based on her experiences, the U.S. is "not better than Russia, it was just a better liar."[79]

Tamerane's younger brother Dzokhar appeared in court months before his trial with his face swollen and speaking with a Russian accent he had not exhibited since childhood. Had prison guards beaten or tortured him? Did he mentally regress under the torture? At that court appearance, Dzokhar's defense attorney stated he committed the crime, thus changing his previous plea of "not guilty" to "guilty." How and why did the attorney persuade Tsarnaev to change his plea to guilty?

With so many different twists and turns on their stories, it is important to research these governmental policing agencies, who are they, who they represent, and what are their motivations and intentions. Who is in charge of orchestrating these actions? Are American citizens being served by some in the FBI who persuade unemployed, mentally unstable, young Muslim men to become terrorists and possibly provide them with the materials and instructions to make bombs? What is the motivation and reasoning for the FBI to kill or deport witnesses after a tragedy like the Boston Marathon bombing? Who benefits from these actions and from this loss of valuable human life? How can these actions be lawful and within our constitution?

D. The Lahijis

In another case, an Iranian Muslim couple who lived many years in the United States had two different court cases brought against them by the U.S. government. The wife was Najmeh Vahid Lahiji, Esquire, a brilliant attorney and founder of the Muslim Civil Liberties Union. The husband was Hossein Lahiji, M.D., a urologist.

The Lahijis had four children, ranging in age from 6 years to 13 years. The oldest was a daughter, Zarah. The younger three were sons. All the children were born in the United States and were U.S. citizens, the only country where they were raised. Their mother, Najmeh, followed the Islamic practice of covering her hair with a scarf (*hijab*). The children spoke English and attended public schools in McAllen, Texas.

The couple was quite generous and gave 50 percent of their combined income to various charities. These donations amounted to approximately $20 million over 19 years. The government took issue with one charity in particular, the Child Foundation of Portland, Oregon, an Iranian charity that helped indigent children in Iran. This charity was not on any list of organizations that were unapproved by the government and had no association with any terrorist group. Yet, the first case against the Lahijis concerned this charity. They were brought to court in Oregon in 2013 because the charity was located in that state, although the Lahiji's lived near Houston, Texas in McAllen.

The Federal Bureau of Investigating began to investigate the Lahijis in December 2000 when their large donations to the Child Foundation were scrutinized. A few days after the attack on the World Trade Center on September 11, 2001, FBI agents started speaking with the Lahijis directly. For the next several years, they were interviewed at their home and offices; they were detained, searched, and interrogated at airports, checkpoints, and border crossings several times per year.

While this case was still under investigation, the government initiated a second case against the Lahijis with regard to healthcare fraud in Texas. Dr. Lahiji practiced medicine in McAllen, Texas and Najmeh Vahid Lahiji was the office manager of her husband's practice. The local FBI searched their records for evidence of healthcare fraud, immigration violations, and more. Any unintentional mistakes of Dr. Lahiji and his wife were grounds for criminal accusations.

Dr. Lahiji's medical offices were raided twice, once in February 2006 and again in January 2011. In July 2008, while the Lahijis were out of the country, the government raided their home.

In December 2010, the government indicted the Lahijis in Oregon regarding the first case, involving the Child Foundation, and alleged that $600,000 of $20 million of donations was in violation of the embargo on Iran. The charge also claimed that Mr. and Mrs. Lahiji made the donations for their own benefit because the Lahijis gave the charity contractual permission to use part of their donation to purchase an office building with the stipulation that, after ten years, the building would be transferred to Najmeh Lahiji's sister, who would then sell the building and donate all the proceeds to charity.

When this case went to trial in June 2013 in Oregon, Najmeh Lahiji chose to keep her hair covered in the courtroom even though she knew she would be at a disadvantage because of discrimination toward conservative Muslims. During the trial, the prosecutor consistently tried to use the word "terrorism" to describe the Lahiji's actions even though the judge disallowed this connection.

The Lahijis suffered a setback during the proceedings when a member of the children's charity who was supposed to speak on their behalf did not because he was to be deported due to his own problems with the government. He reportedly made a deal without the presence of his attorney that allowed him to stay in the U.S. if he would not speak on the Lahiji's behalf.

In 2011, the government indicted the Lahijis in the Texas case, alleging $8,500 in healthcare fraud. At a disadvantage due to the case in Oregon, they entered into a plea agreement.

Then, on November 19, 2013, a jury found the Lahijis guilty of all charges filed in Texas. They were sentenced to prison, must pay the U.S. a total of $3.5 million (in addition to the $2 million they already paid), and then leave the U.S. permanently, giving up their citizenships.[80] The guilty plea agreement was finalized on January 24, 2014.

According to a Medicaid Fraud Report, dated January/ February 2014, Attorney General Abbott announced on January 24, 2014, that "Hossein Lahiji, M.D. and his wife Najmeh Vahid Lahiji were each sentenced in federal court in Houston to 12 months of incarceration with three years of supervised release. They paid $704,000 in restitution collectively and $1,250,000 fine each. They face deportation to Iran upon their release. They pleaded guilty in December 2013 to conspiracy to commit health care fraud and conspiracy to violate Iranian sanctions. The loss to Medicaid and Medicare is approximately $63,000."[81]

According to Mrs. Lahiji as well as citizens' rights advocacy groups, this type of intense scrutiny over long periods of time and using the "terrorism" word in court is known as "preemptive prosecution." This tactic is used by federal prosecutors since the attack on the World Trade Center in 2001, if they suspect there could be any possibility of a connection to "terrorism" even three times removed."[82] [83]

One can only imagine the turmoil and devastation caused to this couple and their four young children. Before the trial in Oregon, their 13-year-old daughter, Zarah, became an activist and circulated petitions via internet, receiving thousands of signatures that she intended to forward to the judge, saying, "My parents are no criminals. They donated money to charity, is that what criminals do?"

The youngest son, six years of age, became clingy and, understandably, very easily upset. The other two boys drew pictures for their mother and wrote short loving notes that she posted on Facebook for her friends to see.

Najmeh loved her children more than anything in the world but, from prison, she was unable to be a mother to them. The Lahijis had no family or relatives in the U.S., so their children had to leave the only country they knew and travel alone to Iran with no adult to accompany them.

The children went to Iran where they were cared for by Najmeh's parents. You can imagine the adjustment that these four young children had to make—leaving their home, friends, school and country; they were thrust into a new and foreign environment—due to no fault of their own.

Can you imagine sitting in your prison cell and worrying about your four children living in another country without a parent and having no knowledge of their emotional condition? Najmeh said she had pictures hanging on the prison walls that her children drew for her which provided her some comfort.

While in prison, the prison administrators saw Najmeh's intellectual ability, integrity, and leadership skills. They asked her to teach a typing class, which she did. I asked her in a letter, since she was an attorney, had she considered teaching a constitutional law class? She speculated that perhaps the administrators did not want the inmates to know their constitutional rights. She never asked the administrators if she could teach that class.

The administrators at the prison treated her with respect and acknowledged her religious holy days of fasting. They allowed her to bring milk and cereal to her prison cell for her pre-dawn meal during Ramadan.

She mentioned that some of the female inmates were troublemakers and she stayed away from them. She just wanted to complete her time, be released, and begin a new chapter in her life. I believe she was allowed to exercise in her prison cell and perhaps outside her cell for one hour a day. She used this time to shed a few pounds from her already thin body and tone her muscles.

Mostly, she read the *Quran* and a multitude of books that her friends ordered for her through a bookstore or online major bookseller because regulations prohibit individuals from sending books directly to inmates. She said her favorite book was *Long Walk to Freedom* by Nelson Mandela because she could relate to the struggles and evolution of this moral, determined political leader.

At this writing, both Najmeh Lahiji and Dr. Lahiji have completed their prison sentences and are divorced. They sold or donated all their possessions and even donated their beautiful home to charity.[84] Najmeh is presently living in England. She has received a scholarship from a prestigious university in Europe to pursue International Law. She is a determined lady, and I am certain she plans to use this advanced degree for the benefit of others. I hope there is a light at the end of the tunnel for this very sad case in which an entire family suffered.

E. Muslim and Arab Scrutiny

Muslims and Arabs in particular, are unfairly suspected and placed under intense scrutiny for any wrongdoings. On the other hand, Bernard L. (Bernie) Madoff was an investment securities swindler who ran a Ponzi-scheme that bilked billions of dollars from people and organizations from at least the late 1980s until 2008. He was convicted and sentenced to 150 years in prison in 2009. Frank DiPascali, Jr., Madoff's de facto chief financial officer, the man who was essential to the scheme, stated that, "… in 1992, federal regulators discovered that one of the largest funds feeding money to Madoff was unlicensed and shut it down." The article stated, "It's certain that if they had investigated more deeply, they would have uncovered Madoff's fraud in its early stages."[85] Note the years: discovered possible fraud in 1992; but not convicted until 2009—17 years later.

It certainly appears, the Muslim community is severely scrutinized while other communities performing illegal activities are not. In fact, from the number of Arabs and Muslims seen on the front page of the papers for criminal activity, one would think the majority of Muslims are terrorists. Nothing could be further from the truth. Muslims, by percentage, have one of the lowest terrorist activity rates in comparison to other groups in the U.S. And many of them—the Lahijis being one example—are very generous people.

To offer evidence to verify the low terrorist activity of Muslims, note that according to **information compiled from an FBI database from 1980 to 2005, terrorist attacks on U.S. soil by groups are the following: Communists 5%; Islamic Extremists 6 %; Jewish Extremists 7%; Extreme Left Wing groups 24%; Latinos 42%, others 16%.**[86]

Yet, Muslims are scrutinized the most for presumed "terrorist" activity. Obviously, looking at this data, we are unfairly scrutinized. Is this reason, in some instances, the FBI gives a mentally ill or mentally challenged young Muslim a bomb, shows him how to make it, and develops the plans for him? It is highly improbable that these emotionally and mentally challenged Muslim youth could have carried out violent acts by their own volition.

These dangerous activities promoted by the FBI, seem to me, to be tantamount to entrapment. It is similar to a young man unthinkingly saying, "I want to rob a bank." Then the FBI pretends to befriend the man, purchases a gun and bullets, teaches him how to use the gun, and supports him as he carries out the crime. If not for the FBI's participation, would this crime have happened? Conversely, if the accomplice was any other man, instead of the FBI, wouldn't a court of law say that the person who made the illegal activity happen is at least part of the conspiracy? And, if the FBI's purpose is to prevent crime, when the FBI discovers an unstable person, why doesn't the FBI interview him and tell him he is being watched? Wouldn't that discourage potential illegal or violent acts?

Three different situations were discussed in this chapter: how the FBI recruits informants; how the FBI lures people into wrongdoings, and how Muslims are overly scrutinized in their daily lives. In all cases, the persons, their family, and their community were negatively affected. Such negative effects seem to be the goal of at least some persons and agencies who are charged with upholding the laws of this country. Certainly, those in positions of authority understand that if someone is engrossed in defending himself, especially against a government agency, that person has no energy to help others who are being discriminated against. Is this part of the motivation and reasoning for keeping Muslims in the U.S. under pressure and distracted?

Even in the face of such oppression and discrimination, especially when masquerading as the law, we must remember that we are ambassadors of our faith. The way we act impacts how others think about Islam. Before we take any action, we need to remember to take appropriate, peaceful and just action, not one that could jeopardize our own or our communities' reputation. It is up to us to make sure the unsuspecting members of our community do nothing to break the law. We must refuse to break the law. Thus, it will not be possible for authorities to negatively and unfairly portray our community as criminals.

Seven

INTERACTION AMONG ECONOMICS, MEDIA, AND GOVERNMENT

L et's begin with a short lesson in economics. Then we will ask difficult questions about when one crosses the line between media ownership and political agendas. Are there or should there be firm boundaries regarding conglomerates who own the media and politicians who govern our nation? Let us look at some facts.

A. Economic/Business Interaction

1. TRICKLE-DOWN ECONOMICS

For many years since the presidency of Ronald Reagan, U.S. administrators, especially Republicans, have espoused the value of "trickle-down economics," which means economic benefits provided to upper income level earners will help the rest of society as well. In theory, the rich will spend their extra wealth in the economy, creating jobs, purchasing goods and services, and thus providing trickle-down wealth for lower income earners.[87]

However, research from the International Monetary Fund, with data from over 150 countries, shows that Reagan's trickle-down economics actually doesn't work.[88] When top earners in society make more money, it actually slows down economic growth. On the other hand, when underprivileged people earn more money, society as a whole, benefits. When the richest 20 per cent of society increase their income by one percent, the annual growth shrinks by 0.1 percent within five years. In contrast, when the lowest 20 per cent of earners have income growth of one percent, the rate of annual growth will increase by nearly 0.4 percent over the same period.[89]

With this latest information, it seems that a more accurate assessment of the U.S. distribution of economic wealth is one that is circular rather than trickle-down. In other words, it appears that the rich become business partners with each other and become even wealthier, while the poor or middle class practice generosity and charity for those in the lower economic strata.

Bernie Sanders, senator from New Hampshire and 2016 U.S. Democratic presidential candidate hopeful, indicated that the U.S. has both the most billionaires in the world and also the highest level of income disparity in the industrial world—a situation that shows the flaws of trickle-down economics.

2. POLITICAL/MEDIA/BUSINESS RELATIONSHIPS

It is instructive to look at the former politicians who have moved to high management levels within corporations or who hold memberships on corporate boards. These politicians not only affect the U.S. economy but also can have a possible influence on U.S. policy that may favor Israel.

As one example, the Israeli government granted a license to a firm with heavy political connections to explore for oil and gas in the occupied territory of Golan Heights. The company is a local subsidiary of U.S. New Jersey based Genie Energy Limited. The strategic advisory board of another subsidiary, Genie Oil and Gas, included former Vice President Dick Cheney, media magnate Rupert Murdoch, owner of Fox Broadcasting Company, and former Republican Congressman Jim Courter. It also included such prominent investment managers as Jacob Rothschild, chairman of the J. Rothschild group, and Michael Steinhardt, a major contributor to Jewish and Zionist causes, including Birthright Israel (a multi-million-dollar program to bring young Jews to Israel from many countries around the world).[90] In a joint venture with France's Total to produce shale oil in Colorado, Genie believes the southern Golan contains "significant quantities of conventional oil and gas in relatively tight formations."[91]

Thus, many multi-millionaires and billionaires (one percent of the population) not only have political influence and control over some major media outlets but also hold positions of power in corporations.

B. Who Controls the Media or Does the Media Control Us?

One wonders whether the media and entertainment field want us to use critical thinking or just fill our minds with trivia or nonsense. In fact, it appears that the media and entertainment industries benefit when people are not critical thinkers. Imagine what would happen if our youth thought and said to each other, "Why should I spend all my money on alcohol and high-priced junk food when it is hurting my body? Instead, I'm going to exercise and stay healthy. Also, why should I waste so much money on fancy cars, fad clothing, and shallow movies when I don't have money for a college education? Instead, I can save my money and have a foundation for success for the rest of my life." Without wasting time on second-rate entertainment, the youth could read, do research on important topics, and perhaps go into politics and aspire toward meaningful pursuits that benefit their families, community, and society.

Much in the entertainment field glorifies drinking, drugs, violence, fast action, sex, and little or no thinking; as a result, impressionable youth want to emulate these destructive behaviors. By trending, they believe they can "fit in," have fun, and enjoy the moment. Only later, after living this life style for a few years or, in some cases, decades, they will notice its negative impact.

Forty percent of teens who began drinking at 13 years of age or younger developed alcohol addiction later in life. On the other hand, 10 percent of teens who started drinking alcohol after 17 years of age developed alcohol dependence.[92] Thus, the research suggests that the lives of those who start drinking at an earlier age will be disrupted. They will be distracted and potentially prevented from making contributions toward a positive long-term path or goals.

What can you do? How can you help the teens in your family and in society when they are consistently exposed to images of drugs, alcohol, and fast sex, and when many movies teach teens not to respect their parents or talk to them about their problems? Many may feel cut off from revealing their genuine feelings, gaining the wisdom of their parents, and reaching out for help when needed. Your help can begin with the awareness of media manipulation. By becoming aware, you can help others to become aware.

Unfortunately, the absence of critical thinking skills among the electorate rewards political manipulators as well as the media and entertainment industries. This situation enables the "haves" to maintain their political power and money while the "have-nots" suffer financially and experience reduced political power. When the unsuspecting public spends their hard-earned money on second-rate entertainment, they assist in keeping the "haves" wealthy and powerful.

In the long term, being smart, well-educated and having more power is actually more important than having wealth. Why? Two reasons: first, having money one day does not guarantee you will have it the next. Many people lose their wealth. The stock market has so many dips and declines, one wonders who gains besides the financial advisors and business owners. Second, using one's intelligence, human potential, connections and political power will inevitably lead a person to network with other influential individuals and, so doing, can become more wealthy and powerful.

By using critical thinking skills, you will notice that most of the media is controlled by big conglomerates. It is easy to arrive at the conclusion that the pro-Israel, Zionist viewpoint is vastly over-represented, while the Arab, Muslim, and Palestinian viewpoints are largely ignored.

Media distortions occur in three ways. First, any negative act by a Muslim is sensationalized. Second, any positive act by a Muslim is usually ignored or minimized. Third, violence toward a Muslim or mosques is, for the most part, ignored or minimized.

One example is the slaughter of the Rohingya Muslims in Burma where, since 2012, 140,000 Muslims were forced into squalid refugee camps after the local Buddhists turned on them. The Rohingyas have been called "the most persecuted people on earth."[93] Yet, how many Americans have ever heard of the Rohingyas?

Another example of the superficial media coverage was the briefly mentioned 2015 murder of an Iraqi Muslim man while he was taking pictures of snow in Texas. He and his wife came to the U.S. to flee the horrors of the Islamic State of Iraq and Levant (ISIS) and had been in the U.S. for only three weeks when he was gunned down by an unknown assailant.[94]

ISIS has never been condoned or supported in any way by members of the Islamic religion even though the name ISIS contains the word "Islamic." In fact, Imams condemn the violent acts performed by ISIS that are rightly despised by any person of conscience.

C. Motive for Media Distortions

What is the motive for media distortions? From my analysis, I believe the motive is political in nature. For instance, if a Muslim (or anyone else) is in agreement with those who support the Israeli occupation or the right wing militant Zionists, he or she would not be perceived as a threat to these powerful interests whose political agenda includes: seizing Arab land, forcing many Arabs off of their property, withholding Arab's rights to property in Israel, prohibiting Palestinians from leaving Gaza, and allowing no financial or economic freedom for exports.

Those Muslims or Arabs with the Pro-militant Zionist view would be accorded press time to present their viewpoint and manipulate people to further the agenda of the right wing militant Zionists. Those individuals who are Muslim and speak against Islam have typically confused the cultural mores of their country of origin with true Islamic doctrine.

Islamic theology is much more similar to Christianity and Judaism than to any non-monotheistic faith. There are 247 million adherents to Christianity in the United States. Judaism has 6 to 9 million followers (depending whether you focus on religion or culture), and Islam has 8 to 9 million adherents. Even with the negative propaganda, Islam continues to be the fastest-growing religion in the United States and the world.

One way to deter people from embracing Islam is by publicizing false claims and inaccuracies such as the assertion that Islam is a violent religion and the myth that suicide bombers are awarded 72 virgins in heaven, neither of which have any textual support in the Quran or elsewhere in Islamic religious theology.

One goal of top tier media appears to be to distort Islam in order to preserve the pseudo-credibility of the Israeli occupation. However, distortion of Islam does not necessarily engender Israeli credibility. In fact, many compassionate Jewish and Christian individuals and groups are speaking out against the brutal occupation of Palestine. Further, polls in the United Kingdom have shown that British citizens rate Israel as the second most disliked country in the world, following North Korea.[95]

D. Deregulation of the Media through Policy Change

At one time, The Fairness Doctrine in the U.S. required that broadcast networks devote time to contrasting views on issues of public importance. Congress voted for the policy in 1954 because lawmakers believed the three giant television networks-NBC, ABC and CBS- could set a biased public agenda. By the 1970's the Federal Communications Commission (FCC) called the doctrine the "single most important requirement of operation in the public interest".[96] If a media network wanted its license renewed, they had to comply with the doctrine's requirement.

The doctrine was enforced until FCC chairman Mark Fowler began rolling back its enforcement during Reagan's second term — despite complaints from some in the Administration that The Fairness Doctrine was the only factor that kept broadcast journalists from thoroughly blasting Reagan's policies on air. In 1987, the FCC panel repealed the Fairness Doctrine with a 4-0 vote.[97]

As a consequence of repealing the Fairness Doctrine by the FCC, there is no legal requirement to give time to contrasting opinions that differ from positions of those who own or run the media sources. Thus, the media sources are able to say whatever biased information they want, with the exception of laws governing "hate speech," which is very difficult to prove.

Congress has regularly tried to reinstate the doctrine. Although, Reagan and George H.W. Bush crushed Congressional initiatives by threatening to veto it, there was a 2005 attempt to reinstate the doctrine, but it didn't make it out of committee.[98]

E. Who Owns the Media Sources?

Consequently, as you watch the media sources, understand that, until recent years, media corporations were owned by 60 separate conglomerates. Now, they are owned by only six, a number smaller than the number of people who sit on boards of directors within many corporations. Does it not seem possible—and even likely—that the executives within these few companies could easily meet to jointly determine what messages they want to feed their collective viewing public? Judging by the similarity of shows from one primary network to another, it is highly likely to be the case.

This could be one reason, when you watch TV or the movies, you will see the pro-Israeli, Zionist agenda penetrating the minds of viewers and consumers. If you want to learn the truth in the news, you cannot necessarily rely on the major corporate news channels, especially in the United States. Instead, you must actively seek information from a variety of sources, evaluating each for their quality and reputation. It is also essential that you discern political commentary versus unbiased journalistic reporting; often, the former is disguised as the latter.

If you research the six conglomerates, ask yourself whether some in the major television networks—Comcast, The Walt

Disney Company, CBS Corporation, and PBS—have chief executive officers or presidents who have political ties to Israel or the Zionist agenda. The ultimate question has nothing to do with the CEO's personal views; it involves how their political agenda affects the management of broadcasting the media.[99] Their political agenda is important because these few companies are responsible for both deciding and disseminating information around the world.

Please ask yourself: Is information from these sources presented in a fair way? Do the CEOs or presidents of specific organizations use their positions fairly to convey accurate information or to further their own political agenda? You can answer these questions for yourself—*if* you choose to employ critical thinking.

While Sony Corporation of America is not among the Big Six, it is included in larger listings of major media corporations. By looking at the hacked emails of Sony's CEO, Michael Lynton, you will see the workings of a corporation "at the center of a geopolitical conflict." In at least one email, Lynton slammed people of the Middle East by writing, "Let them all kill each other."[100] "Israel may be in the catbird seat. Let them all kill each other around the Jewish state and pick up the pieces after they have exhausted themselves."[101]

On the other hand, to Lynton's credit, Sony did produce an excellent documentary called *The Gatekeepers,* which consisted of interviews with former Israeli military generals who described their intense surveillance and scrutiny of Palestinians and treatment of any persons suspected of anti-Israeli activity in the occupied territories.

Arnon Milchan, a Hollywood producer admits to being a former Israeli intelligence agent. His credits include the film *Pretty Woman*.[102] In his biography, *Confidential: The Life of Secret Agent Turned Hollywood Tycoon—Arnon Milchan*, Milchan, admitted to performing an internationally illegal and dangerous act that was kept secret from the public for decades and for which he was never charged. The act was the purchase of "switches"—equipment that could be used for both medical purposes and manufacture of nuclear arms—for Israel's alleged nuclear program. Milchan was never brought to trial because Shimon Peres, the prime minister of Israel from 1984 to 1986 and 1995 to 1996, interceded with the Reagan administration. This is an interesting fact considering that Ronald Reagan was once a famous actor.[103] Milchan also stated that his friends in Hollywood also helped as Israeli agents.[104]

Based on this information, might we not wonder whether Milchan's allegiance to Israel influences his media decisions today? On a broader scale, doesn't Milchan's story give us pause to consider whether the agenda of Hollywood producers is to use movies as techniques and tools of propaganda? It is easy to see the significant increase in the number of apparent Muslim or Arab villains on TV and movies.

Most Muslims and Jews are fully aware of blatant "Zionist propaganda".[105] A number of Jews agree with the human rights perspective, including Bernie Sanders. Unfortunately, the majority of Americans may be unaware of the more subtle persuasiveness of top tier mainstream media.

F. Who Runs Our Government?

1. U.S. POLITICIANS AND ISRAEL

Michigan Governor Rick Snyder returned from a trip to Israel in 2014. He may have been thinking of running for President at that time. He stated that his reason for travelling to Israel was to seek jobs for Michigan. Instead, he signed a letter of intent to share research regarding industrial pursuits and develop collaboration that allows Michigan to share information with Israel. How does Michigan gain from this collaborative agreement?

As part of the U.S. Presidential race for 2016, Ted Cruz and other Republican hopefuls indicated they will travel to Israel. Are these trips ritualistic behavior required of anyone being groomed to run for President of the U.S.? Do these candidates love Israel or do they go to Israel because they are hopeful of obtaining heavy funding from billionaire American Zionists? For these presidential candidates, the stakes are high. The Koch brothers, for example, have offered $1 billion to the Republican nominee for the 2016 U.S. presidential race.

2. REDUCTION OF RIGHTS AND BENEFITS FOR U.S. CITIZENS

In Michigan, Governor Snyder eliminated rights of tenure for public school teachers in 2011.[106] In 2014, teacher tenure protection is up for debate, with sixteen states requiring the results of teacher evaluations to be used in determining whether or not a teacher should be granted tenure, while other states measure student achievement to be the determining factor.[107]

In Wisconsin, Governor Scott Walker removed bargaining rights for union members, and the state court upheld it in 2013.[108] In 2015, 25 states still had "right to work laws," a statute that prohibits agreements between labor and employers that govern the extent to which a union can require their employees' membership in a union or payment of union dues or fees as a condition of their employment.[109]

In these previously mentioned cases, the policy makers have instituted policies where the middle and lower class are losing rights and benefits while getting less pay. Without tenure for teachers and without effective unions, older people with seniority, who are paid more, can be fired or terminated more easily, while younger, less experienced workers can be hired and paid lower wages.

These practices drive down the amount of wages the employer must pay employees. And these practices can be harmful to the people, the state, and the overall economy. As Gordon Lafer, an influential economist from University of Oregon, states, "It may benefit employers not to negotiate with employees and to pay less, but that's different from saying this is going to help a state's economic development."[110] As a result, if the middle and lower socio-economic class try to make their voices heard through demonstrations or protests, they must sacrifice their valuable leisure time or risk losing their jobs.

One may ask the question: Are our elected officials independent thinkers or do other individuals or groups control their decision making? In other words, do our officials represent their constituents or do they represent the wealthy and powerful?

At the Congressional level, conservative Republicans of the Tea Party have figuratively tied President Barack Obama's hands behind his back. He cannot count on Congress to support his programs or bills. He does not want the poor to relinquish Medicaid and Social Security and wanted the wealthy to pay their fair share. But conservative politicians refused to cooperate on both of these issues. Ask yourself: "To what extent do lobbyists, who are paid approximately $100,000 to $300,000 annually, influence these conservatives?"

One can argue that often politicians favor his or her interests over the interests of their constituents. Unfortunately, in many cases, this behavior is reinforced by big businesses and lobbyists who promise politicians financial and job security upon their retirement from the legislature. Unless citizens elect representatives who think for themselves and make decisions for the common good, the status quo will remain unchanged. Financial and job security for the majority of the citizens in the U.S. will become less and less a priority for policy makers.

Anne Marie Ameri, Ph.D.

G. History and Influences on the 2015 Iran Nuclear Deal

In late 2013, the United States initiated a nuclear proposal deal with Iran.[111] Throughout the process, President Obama and Secretary of State John Kerry were under intense pressure from Israeli Prime Minister Benjamin Netanyahu not to sign that proposal. After the U.S. signed the initial proposal, Netanyahu stated, on November 24, 2013, in Jerusalem, "This is not a historical agreement, but a historic mistake."[112] Interestingly, it seemed that Netanyahu's stance was given more media time then Kerry's.

In February 2015, Al Jazeera released an article explaining a top secret document sent by Mossad (the Israeli intelligence service, established in 1951). Mossad disagreed with Netanyahu's claim that Iran was close to developing a nuclear bomb. The top secret document stated Iran's present capability was at 20 percent and was used for peaceful purposes.[113] Obviously, Netanyahu exaggerated and used scare tactics to influence the U.S. administration to refrain from signing the agreement, even though not signing could possibly have led the U.S. to attack Iran in the future.

How many U.S. Democratic and Republican congressmen and senators travelled to Israel to hear Netanyahu speak about the dangers of the Iran nuclear deal in August 2015? Over 40 U.S. lawmakers met with Netanyahu to hear his viewpoint about the Iran nuclear deal. The AIPAC- linked nonprofit known as American Israel Education Foundation has paid to send the lawmakers to Israel.[114] In fact, over the past 14 years, the foundation spent more than $9.4 million on Congressional travel.[115]

Why would these Congressmen be influenced by a foreign government to support Israel instead of our U.S. administration's position? How would they benefit from voting with a foreign government, instead of aligning with our administration? How will they justify their actions to their constituents?

In 2003, the U.S. intelligence service provided misinformation to government officials about Iraq. The consequence was a "mistake" that caused our government to declare war on Iraq. This war caused the breakdown of Iraqi infrastructure and killed a million people. According to a 2003 article in *USA Today*, retired Israeli general and senior military intelligence officer, Shlomo Brom, is quoted as saying, "Israeli intelligence overplayed the threat posed by Iraq and reinforced the U.S. and British assessment that Saddam Hussein had large amounts of weapons of mass destruction.". Brom indicated that the "Israeli assessment may have been colored by politics including the desire to see the Iraqi leader toppled." According to the same article, "Brom stopped short of accusing Israeli intelligence officials of intentionally misleading Britain and the U.S."[116]

This leads us to ask: Can U.S. political leaders trust Israeli intelligence in the future? Can we rely on Israeli intelligence when their hidden agenda might be to motivate the U.S. to stop nuclear deals or to go to war on their behalf? Can the

Anne Marie Ameri, Ph.D.

U.S. make a valid decision to declare war on Iran or any other Middle Eastern country when this "intelligence" from Israeli sources—or any other source—could be colored by politics and result in politically benefiting nations or persons not aligned with U.S. interests?

Section III

HISTORY TO PRESENT, EMPIRE
BUILDING AND RECOMMENDATIONS

Eight

The Cost of War Since 2001 and Cost of Aid to Israel

Let us use our critical thinking skills to answer these questions: What countries or organizations benefited most from the attack on the World Trade Center on September 11, 2001?

What countries or groups were hurt the most?

A. Significant U.S. Growth in Defense Spending

From 2001 to 2011, the U.S. base defense budget soared from $287 billion to $530 billion. This excludes the primary cost of the Iraq and Afghanistan wars. In 2011, the U.S. government spent about $878 billion or 25 per cent of the Federal Budget on defense and international security assistance, compared with 3 per cent on education.[117] The $878 billion includes the Pentagon's underlying costs and the wars in Iraq and Afghanistan.[118]

In 2011, the budget for the war in Afghanistan was $108 billion, while the budget for the war in Iraq was $50 billion.[119] The $878 billion includes arms transfers to foreign governments while an additional $127 billion, or about 3.5 percent of the federal budget, was spent on benefits for veterans.[120] The total cost of these wars from 2001 to 2015 was at least $3.7 trillion and probably more.[121] Does this sound like a democracy that listens to and acts on behalf of its citizens or more like a country focused on aggressive international military objectives?

B. U.S. Gives More Foreign Aid to Israel than to Any Other Country

Different sources indicate that the U.S. provides Israel with percentages ranging from approximately 9 percent[122] to 33.3 percent of the total foreign aid budget.[123] More than $1.5 billion in *private* U.S. funds go to Israel annually; ($1 billion in private tax-deductible donations and $500 million in Israeli bonds.) Americans make tax-deductible contributions to Israel (a foreign government) through a number of Jewish charities. This legal strategy does not occur with any other country.[124] Israel comprises .001 percent of the world population yet ranks as the sixteenth wealthiest country in the world.[125] Let us look at the exorbitant amount of aid Israel receives, and then address the possible factors for Israel receiving this amount.

The U.S. has supplied Israel with the latest defense technology and $118 billion in financial assistance from 1948 through 2014 (in current or non-inflation adjusted dollars, almost all of it in military assistance). [126] Since World War II, no other country has received as much financial aid. [127] U.S. aid to Israel has totaled $233.7 billion over six decades after adjusting for inflation. [128]

For the fiscal year 2015, the U.S. provided Israel with foreign military financing (FMF) that amounts to 23 to 25 per cent of the overall Israeli defense budget. This percentage demonstrates the amount of dependence Israel has on U.S. financial and military support. [129]

For the year 2015 alone, the U.S. administration gave Israel $3.1 billion in direct bilateral military aid, in addition to $619.8 million for joint U.S.-Israel missile defense programs, bringing total military aid to Israel to $3.7 billion for 2015. There is a strong possibility that annual aid to Israel will increase in the future. [130]

Interestingly, foreign aid to Israel is generally delivered in the first 30 days of the fiscal year, while most other foreign recipients receive aid in installments. Previously, U.S. aid was given to Israel for Soviet Jews Resettlement Loan Guarantees. [131] Now, the U.S. is giving expanded aid to include resettlements, in general.

The U.S. Congress has continually and consistently given enormous amounts of financial support to Israel. In fact, reviewing certain bills sponsored by Congress is reminiscent to reading science fiction. In 2013, The Iron Dome Support Act stated that Israel had five operational Iron Dome Defense batteries deployed in the field at 85 per cent accuracy for stopping rockets from "non-state actors." U.S. taxpayers paid billions of dollars for these batteries. The bill states that Israel is ready to share with the U.S. its technology of Iron Dome.[132] Besides the Iron Dome, the U.S. is providing money for Arrow I, II, and III, David's Sling (aka Magic Wand) and AB/TPY-2 X-Band radar systems.[133] I highly recommend you read the illuminating report from the Congressional Research Service, U.S. Foreign Aid to Israel, dated June 10, 2015. This report is extensive, detailed, and thorough. The report is self-explanatory and each of us needs to be educated to understand how our taxpayer money is being spent.[134]

Our Congress has passed many bills that give Israel a Qualitative Military Edge (QME). On the other hand, the U.S. has significant restrictions on its own ability to give military aid to other countries in the region and has to first explain to Israel how that aid will not "alter the strategic and tactical balance in the region, including the relative capabilities; and Israel's capacity to respond...."[135]

With Congress passing the nuclear deal with Iran, the Obama Administration is considering providing Israel with GBU-57 30,000-pound bunker-buster bombs, known as Massive Ordnance Penetrators (MOPs) along with the aircraft[136] to carry them.[137] On May 19, 2015, the Defense Security

Cooperation Agency published a notification of a proposed U.S. sale to Israel of $1.879 billion worth of guided bomb kits, warheads, hellfire missiles, and medium-range air-to-air missiles.[138] Our Congress is even giving Israel our surplus defense material. How does our country have a "surplus or stockpile?" Do we intentionally continue to order and manufacture more defense material than we need so Israel can be the recipient?

At the same time that Congress is willing to give more money and weapons to Israel because of the Iran nuclear deal, the majority of Americans oppose compensating Israel for the Iran nuclear deal. More than 92 per cent of Americans do not support increasing annual U.S. aid to Israel from $3.5 billion to $5 billion. More than 95 per cent do not support giving Israel deep penetrating "bunker buster" bombs of the type to destroy fortified targets. Also, 96 per cent of Americans do not support providing Israel with B-52 long-range bombers.[139]

C. Some Politicians' Relationships with Israel

One fifth of all members of Congress went to Israel in 2011.[140] Do you think they visited Gaza to witness the effects of the Israeli incursion on the Gazans such as the lack of food or resources? I think you know the answer.

Many Congressmen and Senators receive donations from Israeli Political Action Committees (PACs). If they do not accept this money and do not carry out the agenda wanted by Israel, they most likely risk not being reelected. Former

Congresswoman, Cynthia McKinney (Georgia) is one politician who experienced the consequences of refusing donations and being unresponsive to these lobbies. She refused to sign a loyalty pledge to Israel that other congressmen signed and the Anti-Defamation League (ADL) ensured that she lost her next election. [141]

On April 25, 2015, McKinney unequivocally stated that each member of the U.S. Congress must sign a pledge to Israel or become a target of pro-Israeli groups.[142] Do we question the reason U.S. Congressmen must sign a pledge to Israel, a foreign country? Instead, they should sign a pledge of loyalty to the United States.

Some Congressmen seem to be intimidated by these scare tactics and may fear losing their jobs. As a result, some may put their self-interest above the interests of the American people and their own moral conscience.

John Bolton was a U.S. Ambassador to the United Nations and then joined the payroll of Fox News. He was also Mitt Romney's foreign policy advisor and sat on the board of the right-wing think tank American Enterprise.[143] During the 2012 elections, he claimed, "Obama is the most hostile President to Israel ever." [144] He also asserted, "Israel should go to war with Iran."[145] One can't help but wonder about the motive for these sensationalistic political comments, given their timing? And for which group's viewpoint was he advocating?

During the 2012 election season, Romney undertook a tour of England, Israel, and Poland. Rather than improving his global image, he managed to make a series of political stumbles, exhibiting insensitivity to the concerns of some of important allies of the U.S. In England, he asked Prime Minister David Cameron whether he was ready for the Olympics as far as security was concerned.[146] His comment regarding "the Israeli 'culture' that makes Israelis more economically successful than Palestinians" shocked even political moderates with his insensitivity. He never mentioned the prohibitive effect of the Israeli occupation on the Palestinian economic environment.[147] Should we not wonder about his motivation?

D. Pro-Israeli Groups Campaign against Freedom of Speech at American Universities

How can massive propaganda techniques become so effective? According to author C. Hartley Grattan, "An essential element of success in conducting propaganda is secrecy."[148] If people realize the information reported to them is propaganda, then its effectiveness is discounted by over 90 percent.[149] Therefore, the success of propaganda relies on keeping its source a secret and obscuring its intent. In contrast, exposing information as propaganda vastly limits its effectiveness.

In the past, right wing militant Zionists did whatever advanced their goal in the formation of Israel. Now, the Zionists want to evict the Palestinians while, at the same time, continuing to collect U.S. foreign aid under the rationalization of "security for Israel." When Israel was first created and through the early 2000s, the group mentality was "Israel: Right or Wrong." However, both in the U.S. and elsewhere, Jews are beginning to see how secure Israel is and how it has devastatingly exploited the Palestinians. Now, we see courageous Jews who are willing to speak out against inequality and oppression.

This presents a major problem for the militant Zionists. Therefore, the new front on the battlefield is the universities. The right wing militant Zionist agenda's goal is to control political debate, particularly on U.S. college campuses. They are fearful of unbiased debate because American youth excel in independent and critical thinking; they ask important questions and seek the truth. Campuses also have a higher percentage of youth who believe that too much foreign aid is being sent to Israel. These students will become the future leaders of our country and they are the ones who will be running for office and making policy decisions. Militant Zionists are most afraid of young Jewish thinkers on college campuses and other youth because, although they may be pro-Israel, they are more likely to be vocal, organized, and opposed to the Israeli occupation and oppression of Palestinians.

Apparently, militant Zionists believe that critical thinking and spreading accurate information to U.S. citizens must be stifled to ensure the survival of the State of Israel. Of course, this is not true; paranoia, like a sickness, is not changed by the reality of the situation. Therefore, pro-Zionist groups are making an attempt to pass laws in the U.S. that state the

Boycott-Divestment-Sanctions (BDS) movement as well as speaking out against Israel is "Anti-Semitic."

The right wing militant Zionist agenda has the sophistication, material resources, and political clout that Muslim and Arab groups and countries cannot possibly match. Nevertheless, the paranoia of the right wing Zionist agenda continues to attempt to control political debate. There are several cases that illustrate this point.

First, at Brooklyn College in New York, pro-Palestine activists were invited to give a presentation on BDS. However, no one was represented from the pro-Israeli position, and this provoked a strong negative reaction from certain supporters of Israel.[150] On the other hand, when pro-Israeli individuals were exclusively invited to speak, with no opportunity for a differing point of view, there was no problem.

Second, two Israeli Defense Force (IDF) soldiers spoke at the University of Michigan in Ann Arbor, Michigan, in February 2013.[151] Two pro-Israeli student groups invited the soldiers to campus "with the goal of humanizing the IDF."[152] Without acknowledging the devastating conditions that the Palestinian people are forced to endure, the soldiers denigrated Palestinian culture, people, and politics, continually referring to them as "terrorists." One soldier spoke of an incident in which a pregnant Palestinian "terrorist" was trying to cross a checkpoint in an ambulance to get to a hospital. Supposedly, soldiers found explosives in the ambulance; they were "forced" to shoot out the tires and the ambulance exploded.[153] These experiences, especially at educational institutions, are used to rationalize the continuation of oppression, segregation and institutionalized discrimination in the occupied territories of Israel.

Third, on March 7, 2014, Northeastern University in Boston, Massachusetts, banned the Students for Justice in Palestine (SJP) chapter after they posted replicas of eviction notices that Israelis placed on Palestinian homes set for demolition. At this writing, the administration planned to suspend some of the students from the university for one year and force them to attend "training sessions."[154]

These situations on our college campuses show that right wing Zionists are exceedingly concerned about prohibiting freedom of expression in the U.S., especially on our college campuses. If someone who is Jewish speaks against the occupation, that person is termed a "self-hating Jew" instead of a "free thinking Jew" or an "independent thinking Jew who is anti-militant Zionist." If a non-Jewish person speaks out against the occupation, that person is called "Anti-Semitic," despite the fact that Arabs are Semites. For their propaganda to succeed, independent thinking, expression, and actions need to be stifled.

For many decades beyond the formation of Israel, anyone who was Jewish would remain silent because he or she feared that these views could be used against Israel. Now, especially, the free-thinking young, fair-minded Jewish citizens are supportive of Israel but against the occupation. One can predict that in the future, if Israel continues its unjust and repressive treatment toward Palestinians, more and more Jewish youth will become pro-Palestinian.

As one can see, some students on college campuses are already taking positive action. They are organizing walkouts and demonstrations, indicating they do not condone their school administrators' stifling honest debate and implicit continuing support of repressive Israeli policies through financial investments. If we do nothing, then we are complicit in Israel's policy of oppressing the Palestinian people.

Nine

According to PR Newswire, dated September 13, 2014, since 1970, U.S. foreign aid to Israel has grown an average of 30 per cent per year.[155] The U.S. is giving Israel at least nine percent of the total foreign aid budget. More aid is given to Israel than any other country.

A. Majority of Americans Believe Israel Is Getting "Too Much" Foreign Aid

A significant measure of American sentiment has been hidden from the public. According to the survey report, American Public Opinion on U.S. Aid to Israel Report, released in 2014,

60.7 per cent of Americans believe the U.S. gives either "much too much" or "too much" foreign aid to Israel.

In 2014 and 2015, 250,000 Israelis demonstrated in Israel because of rising prices. Following those protests, Israeli Prime Minister Benjamin Netanyahu announced the commencement of more construction in Jerusalem and the West Bank on Palestinian-owned and occupied territory, a direct violation of international law. In other words, Israel is collecting U.S. foreign aid and using the money to build settlements on occupied territory, in blatant disregard of international law and distracting from the real issues at hand.

B. Symington and Glenn Amendments and Israel: Laws Broken

A declassified U.S. Army report titled The Joint Operating Environment 2008, identified Israel as a nuclear weapons power. The U.S. Foreign Assistance Act of 1961, amended by the Symington Amendment of 1976 and the Glenn Amendment of 1977, prohibits U.S. military assistance to countries that acquire or transfer nuclear reprocessing technology outside of international nonproliferation regimes. Israel did not sign the Nuclear Non-Proliferation Treaty. Iran has signed it. Therefore, under the Symington and Glenn Amendments, theoretically, and ironically, that means Iran would be more entitled to military aid than Israel.

If Congress wants to provide U.S. taxpayer-funded foreign aid to Israel in compliance with U.S. law, it may do so only under a special waiver from the President of the U.S. [156] Under the Symington and Glenn Amendments however, foreign military aid to Israel should be prohibited. Thus, Congress is breaking its own law by giving U.S. military assistance to a country that acquired or transferred nuclear processing technology outside of the international nonproliferation regimes.

At President Obama's first White House news conference in 2009, the late Helen Thomas, an Arab-American journalist and member of the White House Press Corp for over 58 years, asked Obama if he knew of any countries in the Middle East that have nuclear weapons. The President responded with a vague answer and said, "I don't want to speculate..."[157] Clearly, she was asking a brilliant question, suggesting that if Obama disclosed Israel's possession of nuclear weapons, then the public would know that the U.S. government was breaking its own law by providing foreign military aid to Israel, unless he, the President, gave Israel a special waiver.

The citizens of the U.S. are smarter than our politicians think. Nearly 65 per cent of Americans believe Israel's shadowy nuclear weapons program should be officially acknowledged. The majority of Americans, almost 55 per cent, believe this program should be subject to international inspections. The poll taken by The Institute for Research: Middle Eastern Policy, (IRmep), collected 1,518 responses, and had a margin of error of plus or minus 2.4 per cent. The research was performed on June 4 to 6, 2015, Google Consumer.[158]

In May, 2015, the United States, the United Kingdom, and Canada blocked a United Nations initiative to create a nuclear weapons-free zone in the Middle East due to concerns of Israel to avoid any review.[159] That means the United Nations negotiations are blocked for the next five years. This allows Israel to maintain a "nuclear ambiguity" policy of neither confirming nor denying possession of nuclear weapons. Former U.S. President Jimmy Carter confirmed Israel had at least 150 nuclear weapons.

In order to protect Israel from criticism or legal action, U.S. Federal employees are banned from discussing Israel's arsenal under threat of losing their security clearances, losing their jobs, and criminal prosecution.[160] In fact in 2012, the FBI released files linking Benjamin Netanyahu to an international ring that smuggled nuclear triggers out of the U.S.[161]

C. How the Cost of Wars and Israeli Foreign Aid Affects U.S. Citizens

In 2011, one out of every five children in the U.S. was living in poverty.[162] By 2013, this ratio rose to one in four children.[163] In 2014, over 48 million Americans lived in food insecure homes; 32.8 million adults and 15.3 million children.[164] How does one explain the vast increase in indigent children within such a short time frame? How can the U.S. government justify spending exorbitant amounts of money on wars and providing billions of dollars to Israel each year when our country's own children and adults are poor and hungry?

Certain infrastructure in the U.S. is breaking down: bridges are collapsing, and many roads have large pot holes. Between 2001 and 2015, the amount spent for wars was $3.7 trillion. Over $233.7 billion (after adjusting for inflation) has been given to Israel over six decades. Jonathan Todd of The American Society of Civil Engineers (ASCE) estimates that bringing dams, rail systems, schools, airports, etc., to a state of good repair will cost about $3.6 trillion (in 2010 dollars) through 2020.[165] Shouldn't we start spending Americans' hard-earned money on our own citizens and infrastructure instead of wars for, and exorbitant amounts of aid to a country that is already prospering?

What about providing more funds to assist our youth financially? The cost of college has risen dramatically. Many bright students cannot pay for college and a record number have much difficulty or are behind in repaying their college student loans. Some of our cities don't have the services necessary to encourage people to live there, and some schools for indigent students don't even have the necessary supplies for daily learning.

Compare the situation in the U.S. today with the early days of the Prophet Mohammed when oppressed and starving Muslims living in Mecca, left their homes and traveled to Medina. The people in Medina welcomed them and shared one half of their possessions with the poor and oppressed from

Mecca. Now ask yourself: Would any of the members of the United States Congress give from their own wealth or advocate such charity to help oppressed people coming from other countries?

In fact, the Republican Congress in 2015 generally had a negative response to persons in a state of financial or social difficulty. They advocated allowing the wealthy to retain their money by paying a lower percentage on their taxes than the middle class and concentrated on writing laws that reduce social welfare programs that benefited the indigent, thus financially squeezing the indigent even further.

Nick Hanauer, a billionaire entrepreneur and venture capitalist, explained that economic prosperity is being concentrated in a smaller and smaller number of individuals who represent only one percent of the population. Thus, not only is the elite groups' economic power increasing, but so is their political power. In contrast, the political power among the middle and lower socioeconomic groups is quickly decreasing. Hanauer believes that if this pattern continues, the middle and lower socioeconomic groups will not tolerate a continuation of this downward spiral and it will inevitably cause a revolution.[166] He says the form of government in the U.S. is not a democracy (rule of the people by the people) but a plutocracy (rule of the masses by the wealthy). Hanauer's views were confirmed by a Princeton Study that reported Democracy in the U.S. no longer exists. Instead, the U.S. has a form of government called an oligarchy, (control of the country by a small group of people).

The authors of the Princeton article, Gilens and Page, report that Americans in the 90th percentile in wealth as well as major lobbying or business groups, more often than not, control the government whether it is Republican or Democratic.[167]

Unless citizens of the U.S. begin to vote for Congressional leaders and Senators who have just, fair, and balanced political cal views, the U.S. will continue to experience: ever-increasing economic disparity; probable involvement in additional wars; and a continuation of increases in excessive U.S. taxpayer money to Israel. These factors will likely result in further degradation of U.S. infrastructure and reductions in programs designed to help our indigent. Hopefully, Hanauer's prediction will not occur.

D. Former Israeli Generals Speak about Israeli Military Mistreatment of Palestinians

An Israeli documentary called *The Gatekeepers*, produced by Sony Corporation, showed historical footage and interviews with six former generals of the Israeli internal security service called Shin Bet.[168] The documentary showed interrogation techniques used by the Israeli government and military, including covering prisoners' heads with hoods and leaving them handcuffed with their hands and legs tied beneath their bodies for long periods of time. Documents showed that thousands upon thousands of Palestinians have been in custody over the years; some never saw their families again. The Israeli military uses techniques such as targeted assassinations and 24/7 surveillance of Palestinians.

One former general quipped: "The Jerusalem jail is the worst. It is old and from the time of the Turks." Further, he continued, "When they walk in that jail, they are ready to admit they murdered Jesus."[169] Another former general admitted that Israeli interrogators were able to get Palestinians to inform on their own friends and family. Asked how one would convince someone to inform on his own family members, the general replied, "We have our ways to get people to cooperate."[170] One can only imagine the physical and psychological torture suffered by these prisoners.

One general told of monthly meetings between Palestinian leadership and Israeli officials during which time Palestinians informed on members of Hamas. The Palestinian leadership agreed to continue this arrangement under the condition that both sides work toward peaceful resolution of the conflict. One general admitted to making life miserable for the Palestinians.

During the interviews, the oldest former general stated there was no morality and the actions of the Israelis toward the Palestinians was comparable to the behavior of German soldiers toward Jews and others who the Nazis identified as "undesirables" during WWII.[171] The general said a "terrorist" to one group is a "freedom fighter" to another.[172] One former general said the behavior of Israeli military is "cruel" to Palestinians.[173] This is the first time former generals of Shin Bet have openly, in a documentary, admitted the cruel treatment of Palestinians at the hands of the Israeli military.

E. Effect of Injustice toward Palestinians on Jewish-American Perspective

Author, Geoffrey Cook, based his article, "As Obama Goes to Palestine", on an interactive presentation by Anna Baltzer, a member of End the Occupation.[174] Several of Cook's points are relevant. He believes the Jewish-American perspective on the Middle East is experiencing a shift, moving toward the Muslim-American perspective. However, most in Israel appear not to make this shift primarily because of the settler vote and by misinformation spread by the powerful political pro-Israeli lobby groups in the U.S.

Baltzer encourages institutional investors to divest from Israeli companies or foreign companies who do business within the Palestinian occupied territories. Some American Methodist and Presbyterian Churches have already divested endowments with Israel, indicating that some American Christians do oppose the occupation of Palestine.[175]

F. Jewish Groups and Individuals with Anti-Zionist Political Views

Let us analyze the motivation for Jewish groups and individuals to speak out for human rights and values. Before the Zionist movement gained popularity, the biblical term "to return to

Israel" was understood to be a metaphor calling those to "return to their religion" rather than a concrete instruction to return to a physical place. Before the Holocaust, most Orthodox Jewish leaders rejected Zionism, saying the "exile" (living outside Israel) was a divine punishment and Israel could be restored only in the Messianic age (A universal time of peace and brotherhood on earth). More and more Jewish thinkers are challenging the Zionist viewpoint. According to author, Robert John, whether Jewish or non-Jewish, these thinkers are seeking the following:

> to untangle fact from propaganda …, for it increases understanding of how we got where we are and it should help people resist exploitation by powerful and destructive interests in the present and future, by exposing their working in the past.[176]

Although we are inundated with media propaganda claiming that Israel is the "most moral state" with the "most moral army," shouldn't we, based on these more theosophical perspectives, challenge these biased sound bites?

It should be noted that, historically, not all adherents of Judaism have agreed with the Zionist position. One group in particular, The American Council for Judaism (ACJ), founded in 1942, stated its mission was to advance the philosophy of Judaism as a religion of universal values, not a nationality.[177] The ACJ challenged Zionist ideology that claimed Israel was a "homeland" for all Jews, and that Jews living outside of Israel are "in exile." [178]

In 1942, a group of rabbis met in New Jersey because they were concerned about a resolution adopted by the Central Conference of American Rabbis calling for a "Jewish army" in Palestine, which was a direct violation of a 1935 resolution by The Central Conference of American Rabbis calling for "neutrality" for Zionism and Palestine. The ACJ said they rejected all forms of Jewish separatism and denied the right of *any* single group to speak for *all* Jews.

In 1942, the Chancellor of Hebrew University in Jerusalem, Judah Magnes, wrote a letter endorsing the ACJ's statement of principles. He said,

"…this nationalism is unhappily chauvinistic, narrow and 'terroristic' in the best style of Eastern European nationalism."[179]

Hans Kohn, a former German Zionist, declared at the 1945 ACJ conference, "The Jewish nationalist philosophy has developed entirely under German influence, the German romantic nationalism with the emphasis on blood, race and descent as the most determining factor in human life, its historicizing attempt to connect with a legendary past 2,000 or so years ago, and its emphasis on folk as a mythical body, the source of civilization."[180]

By 2013, the ACJ had an estimated 2,000 members. The ACJ states that it wishes Israel well. Nevertheless, it views the

State of Israel and Zionist ideology as irrelevant to the lives of American Jews.

ACJ recommends, as a solution to the conflict between Jews and Arabs, the formation of a democratic state in Palestine in which Arabs and Jews share governance and have equal rights and responsibilities. It rejects the creation of an exclusively Jewish state as "undemocratic and as a retreat from the universal vision of Judaism."[181] The group desires peace in the region.

Henry Siegman, former executive director of the ACJ and President of U.S./Middle East Project, was interviewed by Amy Goodman of *Democracy Now* in May 2015. Siegman has been a vocal critic of Israel's policies in the occupied territories and has urged Israel to engage with Hamas. He believes that in order to give peace a chance between Palestine and Israel, Palestinians must give up on Netanyahu and go to the U.N. Security Council with U.S. support and present both parties with clear terms for resumed peace talks.[182] Siegman rejects the "racism" preached by present day ministers in Israel.

He explained further:

Can you imagine if … in the U.S. we had two tracks for citizenship? One track to citizenship would be what our laws are today, but then, there will be a fast track, run by the White House… under the White House's jurisdiction … a conversion program with priests … and who would give citizenship on a fast-track basis to people who convert to Catholicism or to Christianity.

The Jewish community would be outraged. That would be just inconceivable. But that's the situation in Israel today. A conversion office in the prime minister's office, works with people who want to fast-track their citizenship, but they can do it only by converting to Judaism.[183]

On July 18, 2014, a courageous Orthodox rabbi from New York came to the Islamic Center of America, in Dearborn, Michigan. Rabbi Yisroel Dovid Weiss, a fearless man and member of Jews United against Zionism, spoke to a capacity crowd at the mosque during a Friday prayer service. Weiss was quite emphatic that Zionists are using the Jewish religion to occupy Palestine. He stated that, in fact, Zionism is a "euphemism" for leaving Judaism. He said it was his obligation to stand in the face of Israel and tell the Zionists that they are "criminals."[184]

Weiss also stated, "There is nothing mentioned in the Torah that Jews should have a land. They shouldn't even own one inch of land in Palestine." The Rabbi continued, "Zionism started in New York and not in Palestine. Many Jewish people are against the occupation and cry for the Palestinian people. Zionists don't want you to see our cries for the Palestinians." He reported, "Recently there have been some demonstrations with tens of thousands in New York." He thanked the Muslims and Palestinians for giving a home to the Jews in the past years.[185]

Another group against Zionist policy in Gaza, is Women Wage Peace. This group went on a hunger strike in August

2015 to observe the anniversary of the 2014 Israeli bombing of Gaza. Both Jewish and Palestinian women held a hunger strike outside Prime Minister Netanyahu's residence in Jerusalem and called for renewing peace negotiations. The Women Wage Peace group fasted, sat in an open-air tent, and invited people passing by to discuss how best to wage peace. They called their mission Operation Protective Fast and urged the Israeli Cabinet and Knesset members to prioritize peace talks with the Palestinians.[186]

On August 27, 2015, the Central Rabbinical Congress (CRC) denounced the lobbying tactics by the pro-Israeli groups against the Iran deal. The CRC of the U.S. and Canada is part of a worldwide organization that represents over 150 anti-Zionist Orthodox Jewish congregations. The CRC declared:

As the nations of the world are in the midst of a peace effort, the various Zionist groups, to whose agenda and reckless approach this plan does not conform, have launched an all-out war to stop the plan. They intimidate and confront leaders of world nations in a horrific manner. ... We declare unequivocally that the Jewish people disassociate itself from these despicable acts. We have no connection to the actions of these reckless groups. The Israeli government, and its followers and sympathizers among the Orthodox, do not speak in the name of the Jewish people and cannot claim to represent it. Jews faithful to the Torah have no connection with this provocation against the nations.[187]

The last example of an anti-Zionist viewpoint within Israel is an Israeli journalist, Bradley Burston, who is a columnist and senior editor of *Haaretz*, Israel's oldest daily newspaper. He said originally he was one of those who believed the word "apartheid" did not apply to the Israeli government. Later, based on his observation of horrific events that occurred in Israel, he concluded:

> I'm not one of those people any more. Not after the last few weeks. Not after terrorists firebombed a West Bank Palestinian home, annihilating a family, murdering an 18-month-old boy and his father, burning his mother over 90 percent of her body—only to have Israel's government rule the family ineligible for financial support and compensation automatically granted Israeli victims of terrorism, settlers included.
>
> I can't pretend anymore. Not after Israel's justice minister, Ayelet Shaked, explicitly declaring stone-throwing to be terrorism, drove the passage of a bill holding stone-throwers liable to up to 20 years in prison. The law did not specify that it targeted only Palestinian stone-throwers. It didn't have to.
>
> Just one week later, pro-settlement Jews hurled rocks, furniture, and bottles of urine at Israeli soldiers

and police at a West Bank settlement and in response, Benjamin Netanyahu immediately rewarded the Jewish stone-throwers with a pledge to build hundreds of new settlement homes. This is what has become of the rule of law. Two sets of books. One for Us, and one to throw at Them. Apartheid.[188]

These brave groups and individuals have spoken publicly to uphold their values and moral beliefs. They are standing up for their rights and for other's human rights. They want the world to hear their important viewpoint and stance. If they can speak out, we too should be motivated to do the same.

Ten

INTERNATIONAL ISSUES

*"A hopeless person sees difficulties
in every chance,
but a hopeful person sees chances
in every difficulty."*

—IMAM ALI

"With every difficulty there is relief."

QURAN 94:6

There are numerous international cases that document the unjustified use of violence of Israel toward Palestinians. In this chapter, tragic events involving Palestinians, Egyptians, Turks and Libyans will be presented to provide an understanding of the breadth and depth of these occurrences. Please reflect on Israel's long term strategy and goals for these occurrences.

A. Eliminating Improbable Threats and Attempting to Defeat Hope: Cases Involving Palestinians

In mid-2012, I attended a slide presentation by a woman who, along with her Christian group, recently returned from the West Bank city of Hebron. Among the slides were several Israeli soldiers pointing guns at peaceful Palestinian citizens. Her Christian group pleaded with the military to cease such aggression toward the Palestinian youth, but to no avail.

As part of her presentation, she reported that Israelis told her a Palestinian killed an Israeli in Hebron over 20 years ago, so the Israeli soldiers have continued to shut down an entire main street of the city and have refused to allow any Palestinians to even walk through it. As a result, since the incident, all businesses have been shuttered.[189]

In 2012, however, one family still lived there: a blind Palestinian woman and her son who inhabited an apartment off the main street. The son suffers from birth defects, possibly related to radiation his mother was exposed to as a pregnant woman by constantly going through scanners at Israeli checkpoints. Israeli settlers come to that street, break windows, and shout for the pair to move out. The American woman with her

Christian organization asked the Israelis to put a wrought iron guard on the woman's window so the shattered glass wouldn't injure them. However, members of the peace organization did not even consider asking to have the settlers stop throwing rocks that break the apartment windows. This is one of a myriad of examples that demonstrate inhumane conditions Palestinians endure each day.[190]

Another slide illustrated that each day before and after school, children and teachers must pass through scanners that emit doses of radiation. Pregnant Palestinian women frequently passed through these scanners and consequently, a high percentage gave birth to babies with birth defects. The Palestinians tried to convince the Israelis to use scanners that do not emit radiation. The Israeli government complied for a short time but soon returned to using scanners that emit radiation.[191] Israel has built 26-foot high walls to separate Palestinian and Israeli citizens.[192] There are different roads: dirt for Palestinians, cement for Israelis.

Another example of the violent environment the Palestinians must endure occurred during the week of August 20, 2012 in Jerusalem. Three Palestinian youths were walking down a street when a crowd of 40 people began to hit one of the youths. According to one of the attacker's suspects, all 40 persons hit the boy. The Israeli police report, however, halved the number of attackers to 20 Israelis. In a condition near death, the boy collapsed and a police/EMT required a long time to resuscitate him.[193] Is this an example of a just and democratic Israel?

Another incident in Jerusalem, in December 2013, showed a Facebook video where a courageous anti-Zionist, American Jewish youth publicly spoke about Palestinian rights[194] on a main street in Jerusalem. Within a few minutes of explaining his views, police were on the scene and immediately grabbed him, pushed him to the ground, and forced his face into the concrete. They pulled his Palestinian style scarf over his mouth and gagged him, preventing him from uttering another word. Then, quickly, the police carried him away from the scene, threw him into their van, and drove away. Does this give you an idea of the extent of force that militant Zionists in Israel will use to silence pro-Palestinian viewpoints?

At the Arab American National Museum, in Dearborn, Michigan, John Halaka, Ph.D., a Palestinian-American, spoke about his art at a presentation on October 11, 2013. He described collecting heart-wrenching narratives by Palestinians who experienced being kicked off of their land. These Palestinians have repeatedly suffered losses in their life. They are moved from one camp to another and from one land to another with no right of return to their original home.

One man remembered not having any food. If he ate one egg, he considered it to be quite a treat. The extreme poverty of Palestinians forces them to take any jobs the Israelis offer such as building the kibbutz, synagogues, and even the separation wall, just to survive.

Halaka said there is no cancer hospital in the West Bank or Gaza. If a Palestinian has cancer and lives in the West Bank, he or she may be treated at an Israeli hospital in Jerusalem. If someone has cancer and lives in Gaza, without the necessary treatment, the person dies.[195] (A Palestine children's charity is currently attempting to collect donations to build a pediatric cancer department inside an existing hospital in Gaza for children with cancer.)

Halaka also spoke about the Sabra and Shatila massacre in 1982 where up to 4,000 people were murdered in Lebanon when the Israeli military enclosed the camps so the co-conspirators, members of the Lebanese Phalanges Party (a militaristic, Christian right-wing political party) could perform mass murders. One narrative came from a woman who lost four sons that day. Her sons were eating breakfast when the soldiers broke in and herded them onto an open air truck. There were so many youths standing in this truck that there was nowhere to move. The soldiers had taken her sons so quickly that one of them was not wearing a shirt. She quickly found a shirt and ran outside, attempting to give it to her son. The soldier saw what she was doing, so he punched her son brutally in the face, causing his mouth and nose to bleed. As the boy reached to touch his face, the soldier kicked him in the most sensitive part of his body. The mother never saw her sons again. Previously, she also lost her husband in a bombing. She visualizes her sons when she eats and when she sleeps. The authorities have never found their bodies.[196] How can these incidents be ignored by the mainstream press or twisted to make these actions appear justifiable?

All the narratives of which Halaka spoke were tragic. It is difficult to understand how occupiers can perform mass killings and mass oppression. It is virtually impossible to justify these reprehensible actions. How can human beings stoop so low? What kind of mass propaganda could twist a normal person's mind to such an extent?

Reading newspapers and different sources of media, one sees that when the Israeli military perceives a threat, it is not uncommon for them to assassinate certain individuals, who, in their groupthink, pose a threat. For example, there are numerous cases of murders of intelligent men who supposedly posed a threat. Scientists from Iran, a scientist in France, nuclear scientists in Syria, and others have been murdered in Europe and the Middle East. The murderers are suspected to be Israeli agents.

A tragic and absurd situation occurred in Palestine in 2014. Two soccer players, brothers Jawhar and Adam Halabiya, ages 19 and 17, were perceived by the Israeli Defense Force (IDF) as a threat due to their soccer expertise. Both were shot at an Israeli checkpoint after walking home from a soccer training session. Jawhar was shot seven times in his left foot and three times in his right, while Adam was shot once in each foot. Police dogs were then unleashed on the brothers and the Israeli soldiers beat them. As a result, the Federation Internationale de Football Association (FIFA), which is the sport's global governing body, urged that Israel be banned from the organization.[197]

Dave Zirin, sports editor for the weekly journal *The Nation*, also reported that four members of the Palestinian soccer national team were killed in their homes by Israeli forces. At least another three members of the soccer team were jailed in Israeli prisons.[198] The Israeli occupation wants to destroy the Palestinian sport of soccer. They think if they can demoralize and destroy the soccer team, they can do the same to the nation. I believe the more outrageously aggressive the militant Zionists act, the less support they will receive from Jews and other people of conscience.

One case in point: In Israel, Youssef Bashir's family home was taken over by Israeli soldiers when he was eleven years old, but his family refused to move out. For five years, any time Youssef wanted to turn on the television or even use the bathroom, he had to ask permission of the Israeli intruders. One time, when he was 15 years old, UN personnel came to check on the family. When the UN personnel were finished, Youssef walked the person to his truck. As soon as the truck started to pull away, an Israeli soldier shot Youssef in the back. He was taken to an Israeli hospital and, as his recovery began, his father told him, "Transform your pain into something positive." Youssef is now attending college at Brandeis University in the U.S., studying peace and conflict resolution. He hopes to become a diplomat.[199]

B. Violence along the Israeli-Egyptian Border
On August 19, 2011, men from the Palestine Communist Party (RPC) reportedly bombed a bus and a car in Southern Israel,

killing eight Israeli citizens. Subsequently, Israeli military officers killed some of the bombers and then chased others across the Egyptian border where the Israeli military killed approximately five Egyptian soldiers. The Israelis then bombed Hamas buildings in Palestine resulting in the death of a 3-year-old and a 13 year old child. Nine more air strikes on Gaza were carried out by Israel the following day.[200]

Because of the deaths of the Egyptian soldiers, Egypt recalled its ambassador from Israel. Protestors in Cairo demanded the expulsion of the Israeli ambassador. Twisting the facts of the incident, the Israeli military stated that one of the attackers was a suicide bomber who fled back across the Egyptian border and detonated his explosives among the Egyptian security personnel. Egypt rejected Israel's statement in which Israel said that they "regret" the loss of the five Egyptian soldiers. Egypt also refused to return its ambassador to Israel until Israel extended a more comprehensive apology. [201] Following this incident, one brave and determined Egyptian climbed the 20 story building where the Israeli consulate was located, removed the Israeli flag, and replaced it with an Egyptian flag.[202]

C. Violence on a Turkish Flotilla

In another tragic incident, in May, 2010, Israeli soldiers boarded a Turkish flotilla that was attempting to break the siege on Gaza and murdered nine unarmed Turkish activists.[203] In response, early in 2011, Palestinians protested in front of the office of U.S. Senator Patrick Leahy, the head of the Senate Appropriations Committee. Previously, Pakistan, Jordan and Egypt had funds stopped when funds were used to commit crimes against humanity.[204] The protestors said that three elite IDF units operating in the West Bank and Gaza committed human rights violations. Senator Leahy then sponsored a bill to cut aid to those three elite IDF units. However, Israeli Defense Minister, Ehud Barak, in 2011, met with Senator Leahy privately regarding the initiative to cut aid to the three elite units. Leahy listened to Barak but did not say whether he would withdraw his initiative.[205]

Violent acts are committed each day against marginalized members of society. The powerful make secret deals in order to divide and conquer the oppressed. They believe that by controlling the media, suppressing information and fostering one specific point of view, they can control people's minds and actions. Inevitably, when violence becomes so outrageous, our citizens begin to lose faith in the news outlets as well as the politicians who supposedly represent their constituents.

D. Violence in Libya

In 2011, after listening to the radio, I learned that a French official flew to Libya to ensure the rebels would form an alliance with Israel before France would publically recognize them and support the overthrow of Gadhafi. Many questions came to mind regarding the Libyan violence. Why was it necessary for an official from France to fly to Libya to ensure the rebels would form an alliance with Israel before France would recognize the rebels and overthrow Colonel Muammar Gadhafi? Who is really in control of the rebels and Libya now? Is Libya any closer to a democracy with the murder of so many people? Was the goal to replace a colonel who was against Israeli policies, Colonel Muammar Gadhafi, with a government that is pro-Israel?

Aidan Lewis, a BBC correspondent profiled Muammar Gadhafi in 2011. He reported that in the past, Gadhafi performed human-rights violations and widespread and systematic attacks on civilians.[206] However, he said, Gadhafi was actually coming around to Western demands. He took responsibility for the Pan Am bombing and paid money in order to lift the sanctions from his country. He said on the 39th year of his rule there would be no more wars and terror. Then what was the reason France decided to remove Gadhafi from power at that particular time in 2011?

The French narrative about their intervention in Libya was that then-President Nicolas Sarkozy was furious because of Gadhafi's crackdown on protesters in February 2011 but had no idea who to support. Then, journalist, Bernard-Henri Levy, met with the Transitional National Council leadership and invited their leaders, at Sarkozy's invitation, to come to France to meet with Sarkozy. According to the French story, by March 10th, Sarkozy recognized the council as Libya's official government.[207]

Anne Marie Ameri, Ph.D.

The emails written to Hillary Clinton, then Secretary of State of the U.S., present a different narrative. According to the emails, officers with the French Intelligence Service began a series of secret meetings in Benghazi in late February, 2011, with two Libyan rebel leaders, Mustapha Jalil, and General Abdul Younis. The officers of the French Intelligence Service gave the two leaders money and guidance to set up their council. In return for French assistance, the officers from the French intelligence service indicated they expected the new government of Libya to favor French firms and national interests, particularly the oil industry.[208]

A March 20th, 2011, memo stated that Sarkozy said, "France will lead the fight against Gadhafi over an extended period of time and that this was an opportunity for France to assert itself as a military power."[209] The same article described a memo of September, 2011, stating that Sarkozy urged the Libyans to reserve 35% of their oil industry for French firms.

A Libyan government representative confirmed that in eleven hours of bombing by forces of the North Atlantic Treaty Organization (NATO), 1,300 people were killed and 5,000 were injured. Were these killings carried out to benefit the 11 wealthy European nations and the United States? If the U.S. wanted Colonel Gadhafi out of power, why not just concentrate on getting him out?

As a result, by 2015, migrants from Libya are now risking their lives and many are dying attempting to cross the Mediterranean Sea to reach Europe in order to escape the unsatisfactory conditions of Libya. The U.S., France and their NATO partners destroyed the infrastructure and destabilized Libya when they bombed it. Nigel Farage, leader of the UK Independence Party (UKIP), a right-wing populist political party in the United Kingdom, said Prime Minister Cameron of Britain and former President Sarkozy of France are partially to blame for the deaths of over a thousand people drowning from overcrowded ships sinking in 2015. Before the bombing, Libyans were not attempting to migrate to Europe in large numbers.[210]

Eleven

DECLINE OF EMPIRES AND EMPIRE BUILDING

"Do no mischief on the earth…"

QURAN 7:56

History is written by the victors; therefore, it is important to remember this famous quotation, which encourages us to question everything we read:

> *"Why … does truth generate hatred …*
> *truth is loved in such a way that those*
> *who love something else besides her,*
> *wish that to be the truth … they hate*

the truth for the sake of whatever it is
they love in place of the truth."[211]

AUGUSTINE OF HIPPO (354 A.D. – 430 A.D.)

In his book *The Rule of Empires*, Timothy Parsons reviews empires from the ancient Roman domination of Britain, to Britain's "new" imperialism in Kenya, to the Third Reich. Parsons argues that there is not a genetic hierarchy of advanced and primitive societies. He states that conquests occur as a result of temporary military advantages, technology, wealth, and political will. He states that beneath the "self-justifying rhetoric and cultural superiority is the rationalization for oppression and exploitation."[212] He reveals therein lies the inevitable decline of imperial rule across centuries and continents.[213]

Parsons further elaborates, "In the process of developing empires, there must first be an excuse to plunder. This may be a moralistic/divine rationalization." Thus, according to Parson, a ruler or country could argue, "God wants us to own this land. It has been named as ours since biblical days." The potential ruler must also, of course, subjugate the current inhabitants and portray them as a lesser class who are not worthy to own or occupy the land. Other important elements are installing a class system, using divide-and-conquer techniques, and ensuring that opposing sentiment is not tolerated and is severely punished. Media distortions and propaganda help to serve the needs of the empire builder.[214]

A. Laying the Foundation for the Formation of Israel: Demise of the Turkish Empire

"Authority, power or wealth do not change a man; they only reveal him."

—IMAM ALI

The following pages, will offer information regarding the demise of the Turkish Empire, which ultimately, laid the foundation for the formation of the State of Israel. This information will show that any goal worth accomplishing can be performed if there is sufficient individual will and adequate group support. This maxim applies to nations as well as to individuals. Although your particular situation may, at times, appear dismal and many obstacles may be placed in your path, no action will happen unless you make it happen. Those with the strongest will and determination will prevail.

First, let us examine the fall of the Ottoman Empire. In the early 1800s, there was an effort by certain European powers to sow discord between Ottoman and Arab powers. Consequently, the subsequent division of the Ottoman Empire played a crucial role in the creation of Israel. There are varying perspectives on the demise of the Ottoman Empire.

Before elaborating on these perspectives, let us define the word "Zionism." According to the Merriam-Webster Dictionary, *Zionism* means a movement for colonizing Jews in Palestine, either for religious or nationalizing purposes.[215]

One view stated by Naqavi, an Iranian author, was that three *Jewish* men in particular inspired Turkish nationalism.[216] However, I believe, looking at the context of his writings, that Naqavi actually meant men who had "Zionist aspirations" as opposed to men who were "Jewish." I think he may have misunderstood the concept and was imprecise with his terminology, which will be shown in the following chapters.

According to Naqavi, Arthur Lumley David, an Englishman, traveled to Turkey and wrote a book called *Preliminary Discourses* in which he described the ways Turks were a distinguished, independent race, superior to Arabs. Also, David Leon Cohun, a French writer published a book in 1899, *Introduction Génerale à l'Histoire de L'Asie* on the racial superiority of the Turks and their historical accomplishments.[217] His book was translated to Turkish in the first decade of the twentieth century and helped to inspire the "Young Turks" movement which led to the Turkish revolution in 1908. According to Naqavi, the main aim of Cohun was to arouse racial prejudices and weaken the Turkish bond with other Muslim nations.[218]

However, Naqavi indicated that the individual who played perhaps the greatest role in rousing Turkish and Arab nationalism was Arminius Vambery, the son of a Jewish Hungarian priest. He was closely acquainted with Turkish statesmen and politicians and published many works on the necessity of reviving the Turkish language, literature, and nationality. His works captivated the attention of westernized Turks and incited their patriotism. Naqavi believed the common objective of these three men in promoting Turkish nationalism was to use the "divide and conquer" technique between Turks and Arabs, in order to facilitate the occupation of Palestine. Isn't this the definition of "Zionism?"

B. Decline of Empires: Muslim-Jewish Relations

It is necessary to understand the past, to have a vision of the future. Although you may have long term vision of your goals, there may be individuals in power or certain policies that attempt to ensure you do not achieve them. Only after you realize this fact, can you begin to understand the basis for mistrust between people and how to overcome this mistrust. To gain understanding, we look to the past—to see what has worked for the powerful and what has not worked for the vulnerable.

By attending presentations, reading minority-run newspapers, watching the *LinkTV* channel, and through questioning, I have found that Arabs in the U.S. were already independent entrepreneurs in early 20th century. For instance, there was an Arab-owned bank in New York, women from Syria and Lebanon owned linen and lingerie shops in New York City, and Germack Pistachios in New York was an Armenian-Arab owned company. In addition, there were several budding Arab political and social organizations. One such organization had a Syrian social and political purpose. It was kept secret because its members feared for their lives, if it was publicized that they were working toward achieving Syrian independence from the Ottoman Empire.

In this analysis, the history and facts will be presented as I have come to understand them through questioning and research. The facts lead one to understand that many factors contributed to the downfall of the Ottoman Empire and the formation of the State of Israel. Some factors were within the Ottoman Empire and others were occurring outside of it. We will look at these factors.

Some may have a different perspective on what happened before the collapse of the Ottoman Empire. In the interest of balance, multiple perspectives will be presented. No presentation of historical events is ever completely thorough and factual. Please read and question with an open mind and then reach your own conclusion. Also remember: "History is written by the victors."

With the formation of Israel, we can begin by asking two important questions: First, is it moral for powerful Western countries to carve up less powerful nations wherever and whenever they see fit? Second, is this an example of "might makes right?"

As we explore the answers to these questions, please remember that Judaism is a beautiful religion that places emphasis on worshipping one God and helping the oppressed. On the other hand, I also ask that you make the distinction between right-wing militant Zionists and Judaism just as you should make the distinction between radical groups and Muslims who truly follow Islam.

Twelve

FORMATION OF ISRAEL BEGINNING IN THE 19TH CENTURY

To emphasize the importance of learning from history and empire building, a detailed presentation about the formation of Israel, the new empire, will follow. This section illustrates the reason it is important to *never give up* your dreams. You can pursue your dreams and goals within the system. You do not need to resort to methods outside the system or ever resort to violence.

In the 19th century, Theodor Herzl believed that Jewish people in Europe were, for the most part, despised by the rest of Europe. He felt they were despised for their money and he even mentioned their physical features such as their noses. He believed that Jews were an enterprising and innovative people who did their best with the constraints placed on them from countries that kept them in a ghetto mentality. Despite these obstacles, Jews created an avenue to make large sums of money.

These were Herzl's perceptions. However, historical facts show that many Jews held high positions of government, especially in Britain and other Western European countries. Herzl himself and Jewish children, in general, were taught at an early age, the value of studying and getting an education. There is an emphasis on living this life rather than a concern for the next one. Leadership, scholarship, and helping others of your own group (the "ghetto mentality" he referred to) and emphasis on group connections through historic victimization were part of the upbringing.

Herzl developed a strategy for Jews from every country to emigrate to a new home in Palestine where they could be free to prosper both financially and socially without the discriminatory European atmosphere. He wrote two books; One was, *The Jewish State,*[219] (the actual German title translated means "*A State for Jews*"). This book encouraged European Jews to collect $200 million with the goal of moving to and forming a Jewish state in Palestine. He also authored another novel called *Old New Land,*[220] which espoused an idealized fantasy life in Palestine. In the German translation of *The Jewish State*, he described his idea of one people in Palestine being superior in power to others. Herzl developed the idea of a "Jewish Charter Company" to purchase land in Palestine at low prices and sell the property to Jewish immigrants to build new housing.[221]

To make his ideas a reality, Herzl began meeting with religious and political persons of influence in Europe. He met with the Papal Nuncio in Vienna and promised he would exclude Jerusalem, Bethlehem, and Nazareth from the Jewish State. He started a Zionist newspaper and took all these steps within a few months.[222] He then heard from a group in the United States that a group of Rabbis favored the Zionist movement.

Herzl tried to buy the State of Palestine from Islamic Sultan Abdul Hamid II, Sultan of the Ottoman Empire, but the Sultan unequivocally refused to be bought, declaring his people won their empire with their blood and they owned it. He told Herzl, "The Jews may spend their millions. When my Empire is divided, perhaps they will get Palestine for nothing. But only our corpse can be divided. I will never consent to vivisection."[223]

According to Herzl, Abdul Hamid's objections pertained to the status of the Holy Places. Herzl stated, the Sultan told him, "Jerusalem must unconditionally remain under the guardianship of Turkey. It would run counter to the most sacred feelings of the people, if Jerusalem were given up."[224]

Herzl's unsuccessful bid to purchase Palestine from Sultan Abdul Hamid II led some Zionists to conclude the only way to achieve their goal was to overthrow Abdul Hamid II by breaking the ties connecting Islam and Arab/Turkish unity, under the guise of nationalism. The resulting 1908, Young Turk Revolution, and the subsequent overthrow of Sultan Abdul

Hamid II, the following year, laid further groundwork for animosity between Arabs and Turks and the rise of Zionism.

Despite obstacles, Herzl was very strategic in implementing his plan. He created the first Zionist Congress at Basel, Switzerland in August 1897. In a conversation with Litman Rosenthal, Herzl said:

> It may be that Turkey will refuse or be unable to understand us. This will not discourage us. We will seek other means to accomplish our end. The orient question... will bring about a conflict among the nations. A European war is imminent... After the great European war is ended, the Peace Conference will assemble... We will assuredly be called to this great conference of the nations and we must prove to them the urgent importance of a Zionist solution to the Jewish Question... We must prove to them that the Jewish problem is a world problem and that a world problem must be solved by the world. And the solution to the problem is the return of Palestine to the Jewish people.[225]

Different proposals were made regarding the location of the "Jewish" state. According to Zionist records, Herzl considered present day Kenya as a homeland for the Jewish people. British Colonial Secretary, Chamberlain proposed parts of Kenya in 1903 termed "The Uganda Project". Parts of Argentina were also proposed.[226] Herzl was favorable to these proposals only as an initial step. He felt strongly, however, that "Palestine" was the final goal because it offered the rationalization, "God promised [us] this land." The Zionist movement continued to struggle toward the goal of forming a Jewish state.

Franklin Delano Roosevelt's Secretary of Interior, Harold Ickes, even proposed Sitka, Alaska to be a settlement for Jews, but this was turned down by Congress.[227] Although Zionists contemplated Kenya or South America, they needed a land that carried the rationalization for a "return to the Jews' original homeland".

At the last pre-war Zionist Congress, Chaim Weizmann (who later became the first President of Israel) said, "After many years of striving, the conviction was forced upon us that we stood before a blank wall, which was impossible for us to surmount by ordinary political means." He stated that two main roads could strengthen the national will of the Zionists: First, the gradual extension and strengthening of Jewish settlements in Palestine; second, spreading the Zionist idea throughout the "length and breadth of Jewry." [228]

At the same time, the Ottoman Empire was attempting to conquer many lands in Asia, and Europe. However the Ottomans were having severe financial problems. To conquer more land, the Ottomans arrived in present-day Syria and Palestine, rounded up young men and instituted a military draft. These youth were rounded up so quickly they were unable to inform their families before they were sent to the Balkans to fight. The Ottoman invaders confiscated food, livestock, and anything else required for war in the Balkans. One of these captured Palestinian youth was the great uncle of Dr. Ismail Noor, who eventually rose to the rank of general in the Ottoman Army and settled in Turkey. [229]

During 400 years of rule, the Ottomans periodically controlled Egypt, Tunisia, Algeria, and North Africa. These countries were difficult to control because the Ottoman Empire spent the majority of its time at war rather than ruling from within. Consequently, the citizens of these countries often rebelled against the condition of informal rule.

Corruption and financial problems further contributed to the decline of the Ottoman Empire.[230] The tumultuous political atmosphere, in combination with enormous problems from within the Ottoman Empire, led to its demise.

These conditions offer insight into how outside intervention, as well as internal corruption and strife, can facilitate the demise of an empire. Palestine was under the control of the Turkish, Ottoman Empire. To secure Palestine as a Zionist country, the Zionists needed to form alliances with other world powers. At the tenth Zionist Congress in 1911, David Wolffsohn calculatingly stated, "It is our duty to convince the Turks that…they possess in the whole world, [and they have] no more generous and self-sacrificing friends than the Zionists." [231]

The Young Turks did have sympathy for Zionist ideals, but this was replaced by suspicion when the Ottoman Empire was threatened by national unrest in the Balkans. The Zionists then attempted, but failed, to convince the Arabs to think of Zionism as leverage against the Turks. (In other words, the Zionists were using the "divide and conquer" technique.) The Arabs could see the turmoil in the Balkans. (In the present day, hasn't Israel convinced Saudi Arabia to think of Zionism as leverage against the Iranians?)

At the 11th Congress in 1913, Zionist Executive Chairman Otto Warburg attempted to allay Turkish concerns by giving assurances that the Zionist movement was "loyal to Turkey." He claimed that by colonizing Palestine and developing its resources, Zionism would be making a valuable contribution to the progress of the Turkish Empire.[232]

The Zionists, however, encountered opposition in their talks with Pope Pius X. The Pope told David Wolffsohn that the Catholic Church could not support the return of the "infidel Jews" to the holy land.

European diplomatic relations were generally peaceful until mid-1914 because of negotiated agreements. After that time, however, British journalists were accused of deliberately poisoning Anglo-German relations and created such a climate of fear, that war between England and Germany became inevitable. According to author, C. Hartley Grattan, Lord Northcliffe of the *Northcliffe Press* used his British newspapers to encourage military intervention.[233]

In the pre-WWI environment, Jewish attitudes and resources in Britain, France, and Germany were probably important in assisting with financing and credit for the war. This likely helped facilitate the coordination and secret agreements toward the goal of Zionist Palestine.

Alexander Israel Helphand, an arms dealer living in Turkey and socialist revolutionary, suggested to the German left-wing parties that Lenin and his associates be sent to Russia in 1917 to further demoralize the beaten Russian armies. Lenin and his associates ordered the murder of the entire Russian royal Romanov family in 1918 to hinder the "white" Bolshevik and anti-communist movements. On August 30, 1914, a committee was created in New York under Louis Brandeis with Felix Frankfurter and Rabbi Stephen Wise to help Russian Jews.

On the British front, four days after declaring World War I (WWI), Britain altered its original war objective from war on Germany to conquering the Turkish Empire. Lord Kitchener contacted Emir Abdullah, son of the Grand Sherif of Mecca, and informed him that if the Arabs allied with England during the war, then England would protect Arabia from outside interference and aggression.[234] (Was this another "divide and conquer" technique of Arabs vs. Turks?)

In February 1915, the Germans intervened in Turkey (both countries were "Central Powers" during WWI), after receiving a request from the Turkish Zionist office to save a number of Jews in Palestine from imprisonment or from being expelled from Palestine.

Sir Mark Sykes, Secretary of the British War Cabinet, was sent to Russia to negotiate an agreement for partitioning the Ottoman Empire. Neither Sykes nor François Georges-Picot, the French representative in the negotiations, told Sharif Hussein of Mecca, Emir of Mecca and King of the Arabs, or McMahon, his British Majesty's High Commissioner, of secret discussions which called for parts of Palestine to be placed under "international administration." Hussein and McMahon previously agreed that Arabs would be independent if they sided with the British, during the war. Notwithstanding, between November 1915 and March 1916, the Sykes-Picot Agreement was created between the governments of the United Kingdom and France with the consent of Russia.[235]

This agreement defined the three countries' spheres of influence and control in the Middle East if they succeeded in defeating the Ottoman Empire during WWI. One document, which was a draft statement to submit to the peace conference but was never submitted, stated:

The whole of Palestine...lies within the limits which Her Majesty's Government have pledged themselves to Sherif Hussein... they will recognize and uphold the independence of the Arabs.[236]

The other document, The Sykes-Picot Agreement was a betrayal of the pledge made to the Arabs. When the Turks gave Sherif Hussein of Mecca details of the agreement, he formally repudiated it. In the end, Czarist Russia did not agree to a Zionist formula for Palestine. Neither the British nor French kept their word to the Arabs, although the Arabs fought on their side.

Further strategic deceptions ensued. British Lord Northcliffe (aka, Alfred Harmsworth) criticized the British Secretary of State, Lord Herbert Kitchener, during WWI for using the wrong kind of weapons and additionally, Northcliffe used his powerful newspapers to speak against the Germans.[237] However, Lord Kitchener knew the Middle East better than anyone in the British cabinet but he was drowned on June 5, 1916, when the *Hampshire* sank en route to Russia. The circumstances of the sinking suggest espionage and treachery. A U.S. ambassador in London wrote "there was hope and feeling that Lord Kitchener might not come back..."[238]

With the Zionist objective of getting Palestine at a stalemate, and the staggering costs of the war, Sir Mark Sykes told James Malcolm, an Oxford-educated Armenian Jew, that the British Cabinet anxiously wanted the United States to enter the war on the side of the Allies, although little progress had been made, at that time. Malcolm told Sykes they were using the wrong approach on the wrong people and that the British and French governments should address Zionist Jews. Malcolm suggested broadcasting to politically-minded Jews, particularly in the United States, a message that the European nations would to try to secure Palestine for them.[239]

Louis Brandeis was an advocate of Zionist ideals. He was appointed Associate Justice of the Supreme Court in June 1916 and was "formally concerned with the Department of State."[240] President Wilson listened carefully to his advice. His appointment to the Supreme Court was a significant development that helped provide Zionists in the U.S. with a new approach. Having Zionists in positions of power made it more likely they would achieve the goal of Palestine.

Meanwhile, a program for administering Palestine was developed in Britain but this program did not reach the cabinet level because of Prime Minister Asquith's lack of sympathy for it. David Lloyd George prepared to oust Asquith, his chief, and seize the prime minister position himself. Because of Kitchener's death in 1916, Lloyd George saw the prime minister position was within his reach. Using his connections with the *Times* newspaper, Lloyd George gained public sympathy and demanded control over the war policy. Knowing that Asquith would refuse to step aside, Lloyd George resigned in a politically strategic move. Subsequently, Asquith also resigned to help promote rebuilding the government. The King of England then offered the prime minister position to Lloyd George.

Arthur Balfour, also known for his Zionist sympathies, was given position of British Foreign Secretary. With Asquith and Grey out, Lloyd George and Balfour now held the highest positions of government. As a result, British-Zionist relations developed rapidly. Several young members of the war operation in Britain were released from active service on the front and were employed in the Ministry of Propaganda or the Zionist Office to maintain constant communication with Zionist movements in other countries.[241]

(Zionists understood the importance of exploiting propaganda and using international coordination, in the 1900's.)

David Lloyd George previously provided legal counsel for Zionist groups[242] and he met with Herbert Samuels to assure him that he was enthusiastic to establish a Jewish state in Palestine. British Foreign Secretary Sir Edward Grey spoke with Samuels about developing Palestine as a Jewish State. Samuels spoke of its geographical proximity to the British Empire and said that the state "could not be large enough to defend itself," and, therefore, needed to be neutral. When Grey asked, "If Syria must go with Palestine?" Samuels replied, "This is inadvisable because it would bring in a large, inassimilable Arab population. It would be a great advantage if the remainder of Syria were annexed by France. It would be far better for the State ["Israel"] to have a European power as a neighbor than the Turk."[243] (Does this information give some perspective about strategic conflicts in Syria and other countries in the Middle East today?)

The Jewish attitudes in Britain, France, and Germany were considered very important because money and credit were needed for war. Five Jewish international banking houses were already conducting major operations in the United States in addition to the Rothschild's in the New York banking house of Kuhn, Loeb, & Co. The votes of three million American Jews were very important to influence the U.S. to intervene in the war and to provide military supplies.

Jacob Schiff, along with Felix and Paul Warburg, (partners in the German banking house Kuhn, Loeb, & Co.), immigrated to New York in 1902 and helped establish the Federal Reserve System. President Woodrow Wilson authorized Henry

Morgenthau to empower the Warburgs to organize the Federal Reserve because Morgenthau provided generous financial support for Wilson's presidential campaign.[244]

In 1917, with Mark Sykes as representative of the British Government, an informal Zionist committee met with the Chief Rabbi of the Sephardic congregation in England. The meeting opened with a statement emphasizing Zionist support for British strategic interests in Palestine. It was established that Zionism was unchangeably opposed to any international proposals. At this meeting, it was also expressed that Jews in Palestine would receive full national status to be shared with all Jews in the Diaspora (Jews living all over the world). Weizmann spoke of unrestricted immigration into Palestine. Sykes outlined potential obstacles, including the Arab and the French claim to all of Syria and Palestine. The meeting described Zionist objectives including the creation of a Jewish Charter Company in Palestine, rights to acquire land, international recognition of the Jewish right to Palestine, and nationhood for the Jewish community in Palestine. The Zionist strategy coordinated all of their international activities. Sykes, Balfour, Lloyd George, and Winston Churchill were convinced that Allied support for the Zionist aim of creating a Jewish Palestine would influence the United States.

When Leon Trotsky, (a Russian-born U.S. immigrant), Lenin, and over thirty others went to Russia to join the revolutionary movement in 1917; interestingly, there is evidence that the banking house of Kuhn, Loeb, & Co. as well as other sponsors helped finance these revolutionaries. The day before the U.S. Congress adopted a resolution of war on April 5th, 1917, the Russian government signed a decree removing all restrictions on Jews in Russia.

In England, the World War I Cabinet, led by Lloyd George, committed British forces to capture Jerusalem and expel the Turks. Two attacks on Gaza were unsuccessful. Sykes needed reinforcements to the Egyptian Expeditionary Force or all Zionist projects would need to be dropped. Three weeks later, Sykes was told that additional forces were coming from Salonika, a port in Northeastern Greece.

At this time, Malcolm opened the doors for the Zionist vision of Palestine in the United States and France. A Zionist leader and British citizen, Nahum Sokolow, through the help of two intermediaries, was given a Papal audience and interviews with the leading Foreign Office officials. When Sokolow returned to Paris, he requested a letter from the French foreign minister in June 1917, supporting the Zionist cause and he received that letter.[245]

The evidence supports that Brandeis was one of many who played a role in obtaining a Zionist victory.[246] In April 1917, James de Rothschild cabled a top level official that Balfour was coming to the United States and that the American Jewry should press their government to support a Jewish Palestine under British protection. (The Zionists understood the importance of having one unified group to apply pressure on the U.S.

government to support a "Jewish Palestine".) Felix Frankfurter served as the channel between British Zionists and President Wilson.

Not all Jews, however, succumbed to this intense Zionist pressure, especially regarding the creation of a Jewish Charter Company, which yielded political and economic privileges exclusively for Jews. The President of the Jewish Board of Deputies declared this was incompatible with the desires of world Jewry who desired equal rights in any country where they lived.

U.S. President Woodrow Wilson wanted peace with Turkey in 1917, so, in July, he sent Felix Frankfurter and Henry Morgenthau, Sr. to Turkey to discuss the possibility of peace between Turkey and the Allies. At this time, the Turks were massacring Armenians and Greek Christians. Weizmann and French Zionist, Weyl, proceeded to intervene at Gibraltar to persuade Frankfurter and Morgenthau to return home. The Governor of Gibraltar held a special banquet in their honor. Then, all the British officials withdrew. The four Zionists were left alone and Weizmann said, "We fixed it." The men never completed their trip to Turkey.[247]

William Yale was a special agent of the U.S. State Department in the Near East during World War I. He asked Weizmann, "What might happen if the British did not support a national home for the Jews in Palestine?" Weizmann declared, "If they don't, we'll smash the British Empire as we smashed the Russian Empire."[248]

In February 1917, Colonel House stated to President Wilson, "The Jews from every tribe descended in force. They seem determined to break in with a jimmy, if they are not let in."[249]

During the summer of 1917, in Washington, drafts were written of what later became the Balfour Declaration and the British Mandate for Palestine. Work began on gaining American approval for the ideas contained in these documents. Many drafts were made in London for use by the American Zionist Political Committee; finally, on July 18, a statement was forwarded to Lord Balfour by Lord Rothschild saying that the British government recognized Palestine as the national home of the Jewish people.

Later in 1917, Colonel House brought the Balfour Declaration before President Wilson, who approved it, but kept his approval private until after the British government publicized their approval. Then, as arranged beforehand, the American Zionist movement publicly asked President Wilson for approval, which he gave. Prepared by some of the craftiest legal drafting minds, the Balfour Declaration was issued on November 2nd, 1917.[250]

Lord Northcliffe traveled to Palestine in 1922 and wrote:

In my opinion, we, without sufficient thought, guaranteed Palestine as a home for the Jews despite the fact that 700,000 Arab Moslems live there and own it. The Jews seemed to be under the impression that all England was devoted to the one cause of Zionism.[251]

Northcliffe was against giving Palestine to the Jews. In April, 1922, he told his trusted worker, Reed, that someone was trying to kill him. Northcliffe's editor, Steed, who was pro-Zionist, refused to go to Palestine and refused to print information Northcliffe wanted published in his own *Times* newspaper. Although Northcliffe wanted Steed to resign, Steed would not do so. Instead, he and his backers devised a plan to declare Northcliffe insane and put in custody. Steed ordered *The Times*, to disregard and not publish any communication from its primary owner. Even Northcliffe's phone lines were cut. Within four months, his suspicions were confirmed. By August 14, 1922, Northcliffe was dead.[252]

Northcliffe was a man who had the conviction to act on the values he believed in and put country before himself. He can be contrasted with the men in high government positions in Britain who betrayed their promise to the Arabs after WWI.

Thus, the stage was set. The events of World War II have been widely documented and will not be described in detail in this book.)

A. Summary and Analysis of Strategy Used to Make Israel a Homeland

It is instructive to understand the variety of techniques that the Zionists used to facilitate confiscating Palestine. Herzl was determined, resolute, confident, and he understood that alliances were needed to obtain the goal of a Jewish state. The

Zionist-inspired authors during the Ottoman Empire wanted to divide the Turks and Arabs and brilliantly used the techniques of "divide and conquer." In addition, the Zionists implemented deception, sought support of alliances, developed international coordination and obtained financial backing. In Russia, the revolutionaries used demoralization and murder to obtain their goals and created secret agreements in which they spoke in code.

Instead of abiding by their agreements or their pledges, the Zionists maneuvered side deals, developed strategies, apparently carried out assassinations, and exploited situations. They manipulated the media and the public through tactical means, international collaboration, and payoffs. Friends were used to intervene to obtain the support of key political and religious figures. They pressured governments, politically. When their objectives were not met, the Zionists made threats and used whatever means necessary to achieve their goals. An essential part of their planning was their ability to simultaneously coordinate and collaborate strategically with many powerful Zionists in different countries. They knew how to combine this information to achieve their goals by taking advantage of people's weaknesses and vulnerabilities.

The lessons we can take from the Zionist efforts to acquire Palestine can be summarized into four strategies. Any group can use these four strategies to make changes *within* the system rather than outside of it:

1. First, actively and relentlessly work toward assisting people who are supportive of your cause to obtain positions of higher power.

2. Second, collaborate with like-minded people, both nationally and internationally.

3. Third, develop strategies based on needs, wants, and opportunity. Be flexible. Be willing to try other strategies, if the first ones do not achieve your objectives. Respect everyone's ideas and think out of the box.

4. Finally, maintain a laser-sharp focus on your objectives. All parties must agree that their goal is vastly and inevitably more important than anyone's ego and stay within legal limits.

B. Analysis of Political Leaders

Analyzing the intentions of political leaders is critical to understanding their actions. In 2015, Palestinian born Hatem Bazian, Ph.D., a senior lecturer in the Near Eastern and Ethnic Studies Department at U.C. Berkeley, said he believes the Balfour Declaration, (a letter from the United Kingdom's Foreign Secretary Arthur James Balfour to Walter Rothschild, one of the leaders of the British Jewish community at that time) giving Palestine to the Zionists, was not written to exclusively to assist the Jews. Rather, he believes the declaration, based on his research, was that Britain also wanted to maintain control of the Suez Canal and wanted to locate a buffer state in

Palestine to protect Britain's interest in Egypt and India as well as to relocate some Jews from England.

Bazian further indicated that after WWI, the British wanted to train and create an elite nucleus of leaders within their respective colonized countries who would view their own countrymen negatively and thereafter, work with the motherland (England). Bazian noted, "that until today, 92 per cent of the post colonialist countries' economies are conceded to [in accord with the desires of] the postcolonial motherland."[253]

Thirteen

Before 1948, there were settlements of Jews living within Muslim-controlled territory in Palestine. These Jews and the Arabs lived in peace, as friends and neighbors. However, conditions changed in 1948. During private questioning after a presentation about the pre-formation days of Israel, Hani Bawardi, Ph.D., a professor at University of Michigan Dearborn, quoted a credible author. The author wrote that in Palestine there were occurrences when, after a Jewish person died, the Jewish family would bury the body in a grave on Palestinian land and then accuse a Palestinian of killing that person. As restitution, the Jewish family would obtain that Palestinian's property in compliance with the laws of the

Ottoman Empire.[254] This was one way of slowly acquiring Palestinian property.

In 1948, the largest city in Palestine, Jaffa, was known as the "Bride of the Sea". The population was 80,000 Palestinians in the beautiful, terraced, coastal, seaside city; 40,000 more lived in the surrounding area. Jaffa was a prosperous town because of its orange industry which flourished since the 1900's. The city also had a budding manufacturing and tourist industry.[255]

The UN mandate divided Palestine into two states, Arab (Muslim and Christian) and Jewish in 1948; the Muslims, however, rejected this mandate. Jewish citizens told their Arab neighbors to immediately pack and leave Palestine even though there were 11 Arabs to each Jew.[256] Arabs were forced to leave and fled by boats, rafts, walking, or any way they could.

In Jaffa alone, the Zionists shot 4,000 rounds of ammunition in one of many days at civilians. Muslim and Christian Arab friends and neighbors of Jews were thrown off their own property.[257] Because of the Zionist military, 95 per cent of the Palestinians were removed. Approximately 4,000 of the 120,000 managed to remain in Jaffa after it was occupied by the Israeli military. These 4,000 were rounded up and placed in a ghetto in the al-Ajami neighborhood which was completely surrounded by barbed wire fencing, and patrolled by Israeli soldiers and guard dogs.[258] They were governed in this location by a military regime until 1966.

Zionists confiscated Arab orange groves, orchards and other croplands. In one case, an Arab family owned 700 acres of orange groves. The Zionists took over their property but needed the two brothers to stay and work on their own property. The two men did so. The Israeli government then confiscated the brothers' profits in addition to their oranges.[259]

Later, the Israeli government exported Jaffa oranges as a way to garner support for Israel. In fact, many Israelis gloated over expelling the Arabs while profiting from the Arabs' oranges. Finally, the Israeli government began to destroy the orange groves to make room for more Israeli developments. In 1978, an anti-Israeli, Palestinian organization called The Arab Revolutionary Army-Palestinian Command injected small, non-lethal doses of mercury into some oranges that were sent to 18 countries and caused five Dutch children to become ill. This action signaled the end of popularity for the Jaffa oranges.[260]

The anti-Israeli, Palestinian group stated, "The oranges were poisoned by oppressed Palestinian workers and the intention was not to kill people, but to damage the Israeli economy which is based on oppression, racial segregation and colonial occupation."[261]

Today, Gaza is an open air prison surrounded by walls and razor wire. Their water is undrinkable. The West Bank has 653 security checkpoints, with over 528 miles of barrier walls that stand 26 feet high that completely segregate the Palestinians from the Israelis and vice versa.[262] These statistics mean that a person moving about in the West Bank must stop at a checkpoint once approximately every mile and a half. Can you visualize what your life would be like in the United States if you attempted to drive to your place of work or to see your family and friends and you were stopped for questioning by armed security guards every mile and a half? Imagine such a gross inconvenience in your life. Now please consider the importance of analyzing and understanding political agendas.

Fourteen

Empire Building From 1953

In 1953, in the U.S., the Eisenhower administration authorized the U.S. Central Intelligence Agency (CIA) to develop and execute a coup to incite revolution in Iran on behalf of Great Britain and the multinational British Petroleum Company (now called BP).[263] The following information will explain the template used by the CIA to inflame revolution in Iran and, later, in other countries.

A. U.S. vs. Iran: a Template to Incite Revolution

One may ask the question: Why, now, are we seeing so many Arab states revolt against their rulers? Why does Iran currently have a poor relationship with the U.S. when it had a close and strategic relationship with the U.S. and Israel under Shah

Mohammad Reza Pahlavi (the Shah of Iran) in the 1960s and 1970s? Why doesn't Iran trust the U.S. government and vice versa? This section will provide background information to help you analyze these questions.

Before 1908, Iran was a poor country. When Britain discovered oil in Iran in 1908, the Iranian hierarchy later signed a contract that gave control of the oil reserves to the British. In 1951, when the democratically elected Iranian Prime Minister Mohammed Mosadegh came to power, he wanted his country to control its own oil, so he nationalized the Iranian oil industry. British Prime Minister Winston Churchill retaliated by submitting a resolution to the Security Council of the United Nations to force Iran to honor its oil contract. After an impassioned speech by Mosaddegh, the Security Council refused to order Iran to give Britain the rights to Iranian oil reserves.[264] Following this setback, the British took Mosaddegh to court in the International Court of Justice at The Hague where the judges again refused to force Mosaddegh to relinquish Iranian oil rights to the British.

Around 1952, Churchill urged U.S. President Harry Truman to overthrow Mosaddegh; however, Truman refused because he was convinced that diplomatic negotiations would be more effective. So the British waited until Dwight D. Eisenhower became President in 1953.

At that time, Secretary of State John Foster Dulles and his brother, CIA director Allen Dulles, persuaded Eisenhower to authorize the CIA to carry out a coup in Iran. Britain's rationalization was that, although Mosaddegh himself was not a communist, after his rule, someone sympathetic to communist aims might seize power. Eisenhower felt that a clandestine operation would be less expensive than all-out war. [265]

The plan for the coup to overthrow Mosaddegh included Kermit Roosevelt, who was both a distant cousin of former U.S. President Franklin Delano Roosevelt and grandson of President Theodore Roosevelt. Kermit was the Chief of the Central Intelligence Agency's (CIA's) Near East and Africa's Division.[266] In August 1953, Kermit went to Iran with the intention of gaining influence over the Iranian media. Soon newspapers were publishing stories claiming that Mosaddegh an "agent of the British," was Jewish, and other terms meant to besmirch his character.

Kermit Roosevelt's next step was to throw Tehran into chaos. He bribed a man known as "Shaaban the Brainless" to lead a mob to attack mosques and other important sites around Tehran and tell people he was doing so in Mosaddegh's name. Subsequently, Roosevelt hired a second mob and leader to counter the first. When both mob leaders wanted to terminate their agreement, Roosevelt offered them $50,000 and added, if they refused, they would be killed. Thus threatened, both mob leaders decided to stay. When 36 Iranian tanks came to arrest Mosaddegh at his home, he climbed over a back wall and escaped.[267]

Roosevelt then installed General Zazlollah Zahedi as Prime Minister of Iran. The CIA paid $5 million to Zahedi who returned control of Iranian oil to the British. This operation culminated in Mosaddegh being charged with treason against his own country. In court, he testified that the only crime he committed was that he did not surrender to the foreign inter-ference of Great Britain and the United States. Western forces also set up Shah Mohammad Reza Pahlavi, "the Shah," who then assumed control in Iran.

The CIA considered the 1953 coup a success, primarily because it secured U.S. influence in Iran for 25 more years. The clandestine report about this coup omitted sensitive informa-tion, including the following: that the CIA worked in conjunc-tion with the Iranian Nazi party; the coup involved mysterious ancillary assassinations; and, of course, the mercenary mobs were paid with American tax- payer dollars.

Also, in the 1950's, the two brothers, John Foster Dulles, Secretary of State of the U.S. and Allen Dulles, Director of the CIA launched violent campaigns against foreign lead-ers they perceived as a potential threat to the United States. According to Stephen Kinzer, *The New York Times*' Cultural Correspondent, the two brothers helped shove countries from Guatemala to the Congo into violence.[268] A documentary on *LinkTV* claimed the brothers employed the CIA template used in Iran to serve as a model for future operations.[269]

Analyzing the interference of one government in the affairs of foreign countries, one can conclude that a rebellion that is seemingly motivated by internal strive within a nation, might actually be the result of a preconceived scheme instigated by outside forces to create chaos and to overthrow the existing order. (Do Syria, Libya, and Iraq come to mind?)

However, do the foreign perpetrators realize that disruption in one sector has an impact on all sectors, financial, social, political, and religious? Do foreign perpetrators realize that short term gain may not result in the long term gains they are looking to achieve? In fact, unchecked chaos within a country results in mistrust and leaves all countries vulnerable to increasing disorder and outside intervention. Some of these actions have resulted in unintended consequences.

Does the background of the Iranian coup lead us to question the authenticity of other seemingly internal revolutions that have occurred in recent years in the Middle East? Could we be witnessing preconceived plans by outside forces, perhaps the leaders of the Western World, to sow instability in places such as Syria, Egypt, Libya, Tunisia, and even Lebanon?

B. A New Perspective

On December 18, 2010, with the Tunisian Revolution, an unprecedented wave of demonstrations, protests, riots, and civil wars began in the Middle East and spread throughout the Arab world. By the end of February 2012, rulers in Tunisia, Egypt, Libya and Yemen had been forced out of power; and civil uprisings occurred in Iraq, Kuwait, and Sudan. Other nations experienced minor protests. Collectively, this civil and governmental unrest, which continues in the Middle East and

Northern Africa, became known as the "Arab Winter", replacing the name, "Arab Spring."

A review of the information about Iran in the previous section shows we can theorize that "Arab Spring," with its far-reaching adverse impact, can possibly be an extended manipulation by Western powers that began decades ago under the guise of introducing "democracy" into the region.

Yet, ironically, for as much as democracy is touted by Americans as the country's method of governance, the U.S. Constitution does not mention the word "democracy." While the words, "We, the people," seem to be egalitarian, scholars say this document proclaims the U.S. is a republic, a form of government for which the head is not a monarch and the power to vote rests in the hands of citizenry.

In addition, the Declaration of Independence does not mention the term "democracy". And even though this document states that "all men are created equal," the U.S. founding fathers did not abolish slavery nor did they give women the right to vote.

In regard to democracy, per se, Thomas Paine called it the "vilest form of government."[270] John Adams said, "Democracy never lasts long. It soon wastes, exhausts, and murders itself."[271] Supreme Court Justice John Marshall equated democracy with chaos when he said, "Between a balanced republic and a democracy, the difference is like that between order and chaos."[272]

The word "democracy" comes from the Greek *demos* ("people") and means "government by the people." Democracy is theoretically the greatest form of government and works best with an educated and informed citizenry, not one that is controlled and manipulated through the media. A true democracy, if implemented and practiced, would be an enlightened form of government. It would theoretically provide for rule by the majority of the electorate while also protecting the rights of minorities. Evidently, the U.S. has drifted from a "democracy" to something else.

In the U.S. and some other countries, the wealthy minority rules the majority. Earlier, Hanauer pointed out that the U.S. has an oligarchy in which the upper class is propped up by a shrinking middle class and an ever increasing poor majority whose rights are quickly eroding.

An oligarchy, in simplest terms, is government by a few. It vests its power in an elite, dominant class or clique. This structure has been maintained in the U.S. by several court rulings, including *Citizens United v. Federal Election Commission*; this was a constitutional law, upheld by the Supreme Court that prohibits the government from restricting independent political expenditures by corporations. This law, in other words, allows special interests groups within high-profit industries, such as pharmaceuticals, Wall Street banks and munitions manufacturing, to make significant campaign donations and, therefore, effectively *buy* political clout within the legislature. The effect of oligarchies on the world can be found in the narrative described earlier, when the British Petroleum Company (now BP) persuaded the both British and American governments to raise havoc in Iran in order to protect its oil interests.

Does the United States actually have a functioning "democracy" or is it merely a theoretical construct? In 2011, Mark Lagon analyzed the reasons for and how the U.S. promotes democracy. He claims that sometimes democracy is used as "lip service to build support for strategic policies."[273] He also stated that after September 11, 2001, President George W. Bush said that he would make democratization of the Middle East a priority. The U.S. then militarily intervened, held covert activities, and encouraged private foundations to work in partnership with respective Middle East governments as a ruse to promote "democracy."[274]

The revolutions and constant infighting in Egypt, Libya, Tunisia, Syria, Iraq, Yemen, and so many other Middle Eastern and Northern African nations weaken these respective Arab countries. The results are more power and political influence for countries allied with their opponents. Nations such as Israel exploit this power imbalance for political and economic gain.

However, not all Israeli tactics have been successful. For instance, one political tactic Israel used in an attempt to embarrass Iran, backfired. In 2007, Israel attempted to pay 5,000 pounds for any Jew living in Iran (or 30,000 pounds for families) as a financial incentive to move to Israel. The Iranian Jews rejected this offer labeling it an "immature political enticement" and said that Iran was their home country.[275]

Can the "civil wars" and "infighting" in Middle Eastern countries actually be a manipulation in order to assist Israel in creating "a new and broader Empire" for Israel? In support of this hypothesis, consider Israel's relationship with the opposition groups in Syria, which will be described later. Israel purportedly bombed nuclear scientists inside Syria and attacked the Syrian scientific research center with air strikes. Israeli Minister of Defense Ehud Barak subsequently hinted that Israel was behind these strikes.[276]

In 2014, Israel bombed the Palestinian population and created severe hardship for them by killing 2,400 people, wounding 5,000, and destroying 10,000 homes in Gaza causing estimated losses of $5 billion.[277] In the West Bank, the Israeli military bulldozed Palestinian homes and property. One can speculate that destroying so many civilian homes and infrastructure is yet another step in Israel's strategic goal of taking land and removing Palestinians from Gaza and the West Bank.

Another manipulation to encourage and continue Muslim infighting and keep them in a weakened position is the use of the Sunni/Shia division as a tactic of "divide and conquer." (The political struggle for power after Prophet Mohammed's death in the 600's A.D. has become a technique to manipulate Muslims into fighting and killing each other, thereby creating an advantage for their anti-Islamic opposition.)

How is this fact relevant today? Today, Syria is in a civil war. France and the United States provided the opposition fighters with non-lethal aid. The United Kingdom has given the opposition forces an additional £5 million. Germany is using informants to spy on the Assad government in Syria and to provide information to the rebels.[278] [279] [280] [281] These nations have declared their support for the rebels in opposition to President

Bashar Hafez al-Assad's government in Syria, although mercenaries are being paid to fight the war.

According to United Nations Observers in 2013 and 2014, Israel appears to be collaborating with rebel groups in Syria.[282] With tens of thousands of Syrians dying and millions of refugees, one can't help but wonder if this is an Israeli strategy to expand its influence by having the U.S. and western European countries take control of neighboring Syria by breaking it up into small independent and separate territories. Will Syria become a proxy state for Israel? Will the same sphere of influence occur in Libya, Tunisia, Iraq, Egypt and Yemen, and other places of conflict during the ongoing Arab Winter revolutions? What happens if fighting continues and neither Assad nor the rebels win? Then, of course, the subversive foreign invaders win; they always win when their enemy is divided and weakened.

Dr. Ibrahim Kazerooni, during a Ramadan lecture at the Islamic House of Wisdom in Michigan, on July 11, 2015, stated, "In Iraq, massive land property is being purchased where Jewish populations lived before the war. No one knows who purchased this land."[283] Does this strategy seem similar to the original strategy that Israel used to takeover Palestine, pre-1948?

C. Syria: The Role of Israel in Syria and a U.S. Incident in Yemen,
(The Reason the Government Gives for Its Action Is Often Not the Actual Reason.)

1. Syria

The Syrian Civil War began on March 15, 2011. It is instructive to review the situation that may actually have led up to the war. According to the Corbett Report, three major reasons may have caused the conflict in Syria.

First, in 1982, a World Zionist Organization report was translated by the Association of Arab American University Graduates. The report indicated the Zionist goal was to break up the Middle East into unique areas similar to Lebanon. The dissolution of Syria and Iraq was stated in the James Corbett Report, as a doable goal to guarantee peace and security for Israel.[284]

Second, in 2011, Iran, Iraq, and Syria signed a Memorandum of Understanding to build a pipeline from the largest gas field in the world, which is located in Iran, through Iraq and Syria, to the Mediterranean Sea for consumption in Europe. After this memorandum was signed, the United Nations and the U.S. State Department applied pressure to Syrian President Assad by calling him a "terrorist." In 2010, Israel discovered a gas field in the Mediterranean, in the Golan Heights. The U.S.-Israeli consortium would not allow the "Muslim" pipeline to become an obstacle to their goals of being an energy leader.[285]

Third, Peppy Escobar, on a *LinkTV* program, also stated that mercenaries in Syria receive $100 a day to fight. These mercenaries are from countries including Afghanistan and Chechnya, and they receive their financing from other Middle Eastern countries.[286]

Does it seem that in the geopolitical struggle for domination, the projected goal of "Greater Israel" is to continue to foster ongoing sectarian struggle? Greater Israel (Eretz Israel in Hebrew) includes Lebanon, Syria, the Sinai, parts of Iraq and parts of Saudi Arabia.[287] In the 1980's, Oded Yinon, an Israeli strategist and scholar, wrote *Greater Israel-The Jewish Plan for the Middle East*. When the plan was translated to English by Israel Shahak, the title was changed to the *Zionist Plan for the Middle East*. The plan was for Israel to become the "Imperial Regional Power," thus dissolving the Arab states into small states, taking over Gaza and the West Bank, and moving the Palestinian population, presently in Israel, to Jordon.[288] [289] The Zionist plan described seven attacks in five years on Iraq, Libya, Lebanon, Syria, Somalia, Sudan and Iran. Already Iraq and Libya have been reduced to three provinces each.[290] Thus, the strategy was to divide and conquer with Iraq being divided first. The beginning of this division was stated to have begun with the Iraq-Iran War.[291]

According to author Stephen Sniegoski, after 1996, the stated reason given by some neoconservatives for U.S. involvement in the Middle East was the "spread of Democracy". Under the guise of spreading Democracy, the actual goal was not the spread of democracy but the protection and advancement of Israel's interests in the Middle East. These neoconservatives in the U.S. emphasized that a threat to Israel was also a threat to the United States. Now "resistance to the Israeli occupation" is equated with "terrorism".[292]

RESISTANCE TO THE ISRAELI OCCUPATION = TERRORISM

Turkish Minister Numan Kurtulmus, in early 2015, said the Middle East is facing a partition plan like that of the Sykes-Picot Agreement (which was the Anglo-French treaty that drew the modern map of the Middle East after WWI). "The current borders have no historic background," Kurtulmus told a group of reporters. "Iraq is now three parts, Libya is two and so is Yemen. Egypt is politically divided into two camps. Syria is broken into tens of regions...."[293] Thus, we see that the Middle Eastern countries are being carved up, once again.

Yariv Levin, a member of the Likud party in the Israeli Knesset, favors Israel taking over the Palestinian West Bank. His stated goal for a new lobby in Israel, called "Land of Israel," would create a Palestinian state in Jordon.[294]

In the fall of 2013, President Barack Obama almost ordered the U.S. military to bomb Syria because of President Assad's purported use of chemical weapons. At the last minute, the same proposal to bomb Syria was brought before Parliament in the U.K. and was defeated. As a result, Obama decided to bring the question to the U.S. Congress. The American Israeli Political Action Committee (AIPAC) quickly mobilized 250 to 300 people to lobby Congress to encourage the bombing of Syria. However, in an unexpected occurrence, the constituents in the representatives' home states became quite vocal and active against involving the U.S. in yet another war.

When Obama saw that Congress did not have enough votes to pass his proposal to bomb Syria, he withdrew the proposal. The administration ultimately accepted a plan by Russian President Vladimir Putin to send UN workers to dismantle all the chemical weapons Assad had accumulated in Syria. The chemical weapons experts from the UN, led by the director general of the Organization for the Prohibition of Chemical Weapons, Ahmet Uzumcu, from Turkey, won the Nobel Peace Prize for their work in 2013. This organization led the unprecedented task of overseeing the destruction of a previously secret chemical weapons program quickly, in the midst of a raging civil war.

All the chemical weapons have apparently been shuttered and prospects were looking more optimistic for a meeting to discuss peace between the Syrian government and the opposition. However, as of this writing, in 2016, prospects are continuing to look bleak. What could be the reasons for the bleak prospect for peace?

According to Sean Adl-Tabatabai, a reporter with *Your News Wire*, the United Nations Observers in Syria have documented a relationship between Israeli Defense Forces (IDF) and other rebel groups. *Your News Wire* stated the UN Observers documented regular contact between members of rebel groups and IDF, starting in May 2013. He states that anti-Government fighters have been observed moving back and forth through an Israeli crossing point. These fighters are allegedly being treated at Israeli medical hospitals. On June 10,

2014, UN Observers documented IDF giving two crates to rebel fighters.[295] [296] Almost five months later, on November 9, 2014, five nuclear scientists were riding in a bus on their way to the Damascus Research Center. No violence was taking place in that area. Suddenly, the bus was blown up and four Syrian and one Iranian Nuclear Scientist were assassinated. Were the contents of those two crates the explosives used to destroy this bus and kill the scientists?

In another incident, an area between Israel and Syria has been designated an "area of separation" as underscored by the UN Security Council in resolution 2192 (2014), in this area, there should be *no* military activity of any kind.[297] However, according to a United Nations Disengagement of Forces (UNDOF) report from November 2014 to March 2015; on January 27, 2015, UN personnel at UN observation Post 73 observed the following: the firing of 18 artillery rounds from an Israel Defense Forces (IDF) battery of 155 mm artillery. (The killing radius of a 155 mm artillery shell from a self-propelled 'Doher' Howitzer is between 50 to 150 meters. When this shell explodes, it projects approximately 1,950 jagged metal fragments).[298]

On January 27, 2015, the government of the Syrian Arab Republic reportedly was planning to strike "terrorists". The UNDOF conveyed this information to the IDF and urged utmost restraint. On January 28, 2015, after midnight, however, the IDF carried out an airstrike on two Syrian armed forces locations in the area of limitation. UNDOF observed on one occasion in November, 2014 and on several occasions in January and February 2015 that armed individuals crossed the ceasefire line, approached the technical fence and, at times, interacted with the IDF across the ceasefire line. In some instances, wounded individuals were handed over from the Syrian side to the Israeli side. This information helps to substantiate Sean Adl-Tabatabai's report.

Also, UNDOF reports that during the evening of January 20, 2015, their observers saw two trucks crossing from the Syrian side to the Israeli side, where they were received by IDF personnel. The trucks were loaded with sacks before returning to the Syrian side. Furthermore, on at least four occasions in February, UN personnel saw vehicles, including small trucks, crossing the ceasefire line from the Syrian side and approaching the technical fence. On one occasion, several vehicles, including some with anti-aircraft guns mounted on the back, were seen parked next to the technical fence.[299]

During the UNDOF reporting period, the IDF deployed the Iron dome defense system between February 3 and 10, 2015. On one occasion, a multiple-launch rocket system was installed, in addition to maintaining the intermittent presence of 155 mm artillery on the Israeli side within 10 km of the ceasefire line.[300]

Then on August 29, 2015, the Centre for Research on Globalization documented that Israeli commanders were killed within Al Nusra (is a known terrorist group) ranks inside Syria.[301] The Israeli commanders were killed during airstrikes on terrorist positions in the southern province of Daraa, a city in southwest Syria, by Syrian government airstrikes. Not surprisingly, the remains of some bombs found in Syria had Hebrew writing on them.[302] For a considerable period of time, the Syrian government has been telling the United Nations that Israel is directing and helping the opposition in Syria; however, neither the UN, nor any other world body, has done anything about this situation.

In 2016, the U.S. and Russia are attempting to broker a ceasefire in Syria because ISIS, a terrorist group, is continuing to gain more land inside Syria and Iraq and consequently, millions of refugees are pouring into Europe.

While the U.S. and Russia are attempting to be constructive, in the midst of this chaos, Israeli Prime Minister Benjamin Netanyahu has for years, advocated an independent Kurdistan where Kurds would control the northern region.[303] Not surprisingly, on March 17, 2016, Kurds in northern Syria announced they are declaring a de facto federal region.[304] This announcement triggered fears that a Kurdish federal unit would lead to a partition of the country. Is the Kurdish federal unit part of implementing the Yinon Plan, to dissolve larger Arab states into smaller states? Is this reminiscent of the divide and conquer technique used by Europe after WWI?

2. YEMEN

Another questionable occurrence happened before the end of the Islamic holy month of Ramadan in August 2013. The U.S.

administration publicized the possibility of violence toward U.S. embassies in the Middle East, so they temporarily closed 19 or 20 embassies (depending on the specific media source) in the Middle East and North Africa. The reason given to the American public for temporarily closing the embassies was that communication was intercepted, between Al Qaeda fighters.[305]

Could the real reason have been the knowledge that the U.S. carried out nine drone strikes on Yemen during the two weeks prior to the U.S. shutting down our embassies?[306] In fact, this was the actual reason for the closure of the embassies and was later confirmed by the Drones Team, not by the media; the Team verified that U.S. drones killed a total of 31 to 49 people in Yemen, of which six or seven were civilians and three were children.[307] Was the conversation of Al Qaeda related to the drone killings? Was the U.S. government expecting retaliation due to these civilian killings? Is this yet another example of the administration giving an explanation for an action which is not the real reason?

We have briefly looked at occurrences in two countries and analyzed purported reasons given to the public versus the actual ones. Can you imagine the information that would be gleaned if the events in other countries in the Middle East could be reviewed in more depth?

a. Double Standards
Let us look at some double standards that are prevalent in Israel and sometimes in the U.S. While Israel breaks international

laws and discriminates against its Palestinian population, no action is taken by the rest of the world. Close to the Israeli elections in 2015, Prime Minister Netanyahu declared "there will be no Palestinian State." He argued that the Palestinian National Authority, an interim government of the Gaza Strip, and Hamas won't recognize the State of Israel and used this as a rationalization for refusing to negotiate a peace treaty. It is ironic that Netanyahu denigrated the Palestinians for their stance but he used the same rationale for refusing to enter into peace talks?

In another example, Netanyahu attempted to stop the nuclear deal with Iran that would bring peace by insisting that as part of the deal, Iran must agree to recognize the State of Israel. Interestingly, Netanyahu and Ehud Barak, former Defense Minister of Israel, allegedly had plans to bomb Iran in 2010, 2011, and 2012.[308]

ISIS is a terrorist group and is rightly ridiculed and despised by any person of conscience. One of the reasons the group is so despicable is that they behead and torture people who disagree with them. Along the same line, Avigdor Liberman, Foreign Minister of Israel, calls for beheading any Arab-Israeli whom he considers disloyal to the State of Israel.[309] So is this not another case of the proverbial pot calling the kettle "black"?

The United States has strict laws that prohibit terrorism or providing material support to a terrorist group. The penalty for conviction on charge of terrorism could be life imprisonment or death. However, since May 2013, it has been alleged by UN

Observers, that Israel is helping Al Nusra, a terrorist group, in Syria. Yet, Israel continues to receive more and more military aid from the U.S., while helping a terrorist organization and having nuclear weapons power without signing a Nuclear Non-Proliferation Treaty, in contradiction of the Symington and Glen Amendments.

As previously mentioned, on November 9, 2014, Iranian Scientists travelling by bus to reach a science research center in Damascus were bombed and all the scientists were killed. Also, it was documented that in a separate incident, Israeli commanders were killed by a Syrian government airstrike on terrorist positions.[310] What is the reason these Israeli actions were not considered crimes against humanity? Why are there no repercussions against Israel for its illegal actions?

Perhaps the answer lies in powerful and politically motivated, pro-Israeli groups who exert significant financial and psychological influence over U.S. lawmakers. It is a fact that politicians who accept money from lobbyists are generally more receptive to the aims and ideals of the organizations providing the money. Yet, some politicians don't seem to have much choice, especially when approached by strong-arm special interest groups.

If a U.S. Congressman or Senator refuses to take money from a particular organization or chooses not to support the interests of such an organization in the legislature, he or she may run the risk of not being re-elected. Is this balanced government by the majority of the people, a democracy by the people and for the people or an oligarchy?

According to surveys taken in the U.S. in 2015, the majority of people believe the U.S. Congress is giving too much aid to Israel. Nevertheless, Congress listens to the Pro-Israeli lobbyists instead of the American majority. Is this a double standard?

Additional double standards include the *Charlie Hebdo* tragedy, in Paris, France. *Charlie Hebdo,* a weekly satirical magazine published in France, features cartoons, reports, polemics, and jokes. The magazine published anti-Islamic cartoons and articles but these cartoons and articles are protected under the law of "freedom of speech." On the other hand, Zionists groups are attempting to implement laws that would make speaking the truth about militant Zionism at a university equivalent to expressing "anti-Semitic, hate speech." Israeli soldiers can come to universities in the U.S. and call civilian Palestinians "terrorists," but that is not considered "hate speech."

Major policy changes in Congress after September 11, 2001, became more repressive to U.S. citizens' rights, in general, and to Arab and Muslims and other marginalized groups in particular. In this regard, in 2013, Edward Snowden, an American privacy activist and former CIA employee, divulged that the U.S. National Security Agency (NSA) has the capacity to tap into citizens' emails and phone conversations at the agency's discretion. Snowden's remarks reveal that privacy rights of ordinary citizens can be violated,[311] which, of course, is contrary to our constitutionally, guaranteed right to privacy.

As a result of Snowden exposing this information, the U.S. government has called Snowden a traitor and charged him with espionage for revealing to U.S. citizens and foreign countries that the U.S. government was spying on them. After this information was publicly disseminated, President Obama rationalized the NSA's actions by saying, "All countries collect intelligence."[312] Ironically, at that time, the U.S. was meeting with China to tell China to stop cyber spying on the U.S. In turn, China retorted that the U.S. was spying on them. Is this claim not a double standard?

Another example of the double standard is that, in the past, the U.S. has offered asylum to human rights activists from Russia and China. Counter to past behavior, the U.S. administration attempted to pressure other countries to stop offering asylum to Edward Snowden. The U.S. government went so far as to make threats and even stopped a plane carrying Bolivia's President Evo Morales, from landing in Lisbon, Portugal, for refueling. The plane was forced to land in Austria because the U.S. government thought Snowden was on board.[313]

At times, the majority of people in a country can be manipulated by foreign interference without knowing it. For example, in 2013, held massive demonstrations were held in Egypt and, with the help of the Egyptian army, President Mohamed Morsi was toppled. At that point, President Obama stated that the U.S. was not taking sides with the military overthrow. However, documents obtained by the Investigative Reporting program at the University of California, Berkeley showed that U.S. channeled funding for the Middle East through a State Department program through NGO's. This program was theoretically intended to promote democracy in the Middle East, but, inevitably, it supported activists and politicians who incited unrest and violence in Egypt.[314]

The question that Americans must ask is this: Why does the U.S. government say it wants other countries to act fairly with us, while, at the same time, it engages in actions in other countries that our government would deem to be unfair or unacceptable if used on us? Is this attitude and action conducive to the principles of a democratic society? Is it not the ultimate double standard? Can the U.S. or Israeli government do whatever it wants because the governments are militarily more advanced?

Whether by the NSA, FBI, or the IRS, Muslims feel pressured or attacked in their everyday life. No longer can people who follow the religion of Islam feel safe inside their houses of worship because of unnecessary and needless surveillance inside and outside our mosques, and by men and women posing to be new converts or friends. Spreading damaging and inaccurate information about Muslims and Arabs in the U.S., and causing discrimination, appears to be a microcosm of the political agenda of right wing militant Zionists in Israel. Does this make one wonder whether the people who are actually in charge in the U.S., are the same ones who have power in Israel?

Fifteen

Historic Treatment of Racial Groups and "Outgroups"

Racial issues have been a problem from the inception of both Israeli society and the United States. Let us look more deeply at the racial issues that divide both countries.

A. Israel

From Israel's conception, Jews from anywhere in the world were theoretically welcome to live in Israel. However, the reality is actually much different from the spoken word. For a moment, let us fast forward to 2015. Israeli Prime Minister Netanyahu called on *European* Jews to come to Israel for their safety, after the Charlie Hebdo tragedy, early in 2015; then few days later, he called on *all* Jews to come to Israel.[315] In contrast, the reality is the Israeli government is deporting Ethiopian Jews and holding many for deportation; these Ethiopian Jews are treated as second class citizens or worse.

In 2015, because of the Israeli government's discriminatory treatment toward Ethiopian Jews, and after two police officers beat up an Ethiopian IDF soldier, Israel experienced rioting and demonstrations.[316] In Tel Aviv, thousands demonstrated against police harassment, police brutality and discrimination; 57 officers were injured, 12 protesters were injured and 43 were arrested. There are 135,000 Ethiopian Jews in Israel and they comprise less than two per cent of the population. Racial profiling and over-policing have caused bitter feelings for many in the Ethiopian community.[317] The Israeli government also discriminates against Bedouins, Palestinian Christians, and of course, Palestinian Muslims, who are on the lowest rung of the ladder.

B. United States

Racial issues were also present in the U.S. even at the time of constructing the Constitution. Reviewing our U.S. history with the uncensored truth, we see that the Declaration of Independence from England, states: "All men are created equal." Yet, viewing three different sections of the U.S. Constitution, the "founding fathers" 'implied' or 'understood' a compromise made with states whose economy flourished due to the slave trade. First, in Article I, Section 2, Clause 3, regarding Representation and direct taxes; it was implied that African-Americans were 3/5's of a person when it came to representation and collecting direct taxes. Quasi-laws were instituted to protect the elitist class and control the lowest socio-economic class. The second incidence where slavery was implied or understood was in Article I, Section 9, Clause 1, which implied the slave trade could not be prohibited by Congress prior to 1808 and that a tax or duty per "importation" (slave), could not exceed $10.00. The third time slavery was understood was in Article IV, Section 2, and Clause 3, referring to the "fugitive slave law". This clause stated that "any person (slave) escaping to another state, could not be discharged from his duty, but shall be delivered upon claim of party to whom service or labor is due."[318]

What does this mean? It means that even in the U.S. Constitution, the implication was that all men were *not* created equal. Those in power manipulated the law to favor Caucasians, majority Christian and minority Jewish slave owners. The "under class or labor class", was comprised of "slaves" or African Americans. If you fast forward to contemporary U.S, the power structure now consists of Caucasians, right wing Zionist elite, and some Christians.

Prior to the Civil War, African slaves were physically beaten or lynched to invoke fear in the "out-group" and to increase their productivity, so they would "know their place". Today, sophisticated methods include the use of mass propaganda by repetition in order "to demoralize the marginal group" psychologically so they "know their place". The reason to control this "outside group," or "other," is to form an "underclass" of laborers and poor to perform the menial work and fill the slots of the armed forces.

Looking at contemporary U.S. racial relations, you will perceive many young African American men being abused or killed by Caucasian police officers. If you recall cities such as Ferguson and Baltimore, you will remember riots due to injustice and maltreatment based on race. This is disturbingly similar to how the Israeli military treats Palestinians. Also, one cannot help but notice the racial inequality in the U.S. prison system.

Furthermore, current propaganda and manipulation of underrepresented and marginalized minority groups includes the statement publicizing, "College is not for everyone". But who is behind this statement? College is for 99% of Americans. College is the key to leaving the underclass, reducing stress in your life, improving your health, and making much more money than if you do not have a college education. You frequently see in the media, information about the "high cost" of college, today. Please reflect on this statement. Whatever the financial cost of college, the cost of not getting a college education is much more detrimental to your health, wealth, and welfare across your lifespan. On average, graduating from college allows one to make $1,000,000 more during his or her lifetime, compared with one who does not graduate from college.[319] This is one reason President Obama is attempting to pass a bill for a "no charge" education at community colleges in the U.S.

Please make the connection with the title of this book. Let us awaken from our sleep or passivity. Can we get out of our comfort zone and take a risk to move beyond our situation to positions that are new and uncomfortable? It is necessary to move out of our comfort zone, reach out to others and work with a sharp focus toward our goals. Whether or not we feel valued by society, have the courage to work toward bettering society.

We need to push past our resistance and pain. We can release the rope that we think is insurmountable and holding us back. *It* is not. Perhaps memories from our youth or our conversation with ourselves prevent us from accomplishing our goals. Instead, we can change our conversation to one that is supportive and positive instead of negative. Each person has a talent that can be used to help their fellow human being. I guarantee that if we do nothing, the situation will get worse. What suggestions can I offer?

Sixteen

ACCEPT THE CHALLENGE

The following section presents ideas to motivate us to see ourselves from a unique perspective. You are urged to accept the challenge to motivate yourself and each other. This chapter begins with a true story about a young boy in Lebanon. After the true story, we will offer ideas to help you think of yourself in a positive and optimistic manner. Hopefully, this chapter will better prepare us to work toward the *solutions* offered in future chapters. If others are motivated to speak out for their values, we, too, have the power to speak for ours.

A. Determination at the Individual Level

First, is a true story about an elementary school boy from Lebanon who had the motivation and desire to accept a challenge. Please see if you can visualize yourself in his story and if you can glean a message from his life and apply it to your life.

Hassan was in the second grade at a private school in Lebanon. He loved soccer but hated schoolwork. In fact, he received zeroes on all homework assignments and tests because he never did his homework, nor did he study. One day at school, he received yet another test with a grade of "zero". Seeing this grade, a young boy who sat next to him in class, called him a *hmar* (Arabic word for "jackass"). Hassan, felt extremely humiliated and angry. He turned around and punched the boy in the nose so hard, that the youngster's nose started bleeding, profusely. Because of this act of violence, Hassan was kicked out of class, sent to the principal's office, and suspended for three days. During these three days, Hassan determined he would succeed in his classwork, so he asked his older brother to help him study for his exams.

On the next exam, Hassan received a 100 per cent. Unexpectedly, his teacher approached his desk and slapped him very hard across the face and accused him of cheating. Hassan was shocked and extremely upset. He went directly home and informed his mother. The next day, his mother marched forcefully to school and warned the principal if the teacher ever touched her son again, she would, at the very least, make sure he lost his job. The teacher explained to the boy's mother and the principal that it was the first time Hassan ever received a grade higher than a zero on a test, so he thought

Hassan cheated; however, his mother was not impressed with the teacher's rationalization.

Hassan accepted the challenge. He was not discouraged, did not feel defeated and continued his progress until he became the highest performing student, in all his classes. In fact, at 16 years of age, he won scholarships to three different universities in the United States. In college, he continued to outperform his classmates. After graduating and later in his profession, he went on to invent several products, bought and sold properties, built a multi-million dollar financial empire, and to this day, helps the broader community.

What can we learn from this man? First, he used his anger and humiliation to initiate a positive change within himself. Second, he asked for help from a person he knew, trusted and cared about his welfare (his older brother). Third, he knew that appropriate behavior was rightfully to be expected from authority and he refused to accept abuse. He fought back with his intellect and creativity. He accepted the challenge when he was in the second grade and continues to foster leadership and determination today.

Hassan made a memorable statement that I will always remember: "The only thing that differentiates you from anyone else is your brain. How you use your brain to challenge yourself will make all the difference." Hassan is charitable to those in need and is a wonderful role model. His success story is a good example for our youth. Think about it, if one boy from Lebanon who received zeros on all his exams and never did his homework can become a leader in our community, an inventor, and have a vast financial empire, what do you think our community could achieve if we used our potential and worked together to help one another?

Although Hassan may not have had a written plan in the second grade, he knew he needed to do his best and achieve high grades. Later in life, he developed written plans to achieve his objectives and ensure his success. In other words, he created a vision for himself.

Hassan used his intellect, his motivation, creativity and determination. These factors plus discipline resulted in raising his self-esteem; his ability to accept help from others, help himself and inevitably, the ability to help others.

B. *"You Can Heal Your Life"*

Louise Hay

In her book, *"You Can Heal Your Life"*, author, Louise Hay, offers suggestions for raising self-esteem. She emphasizes that you need to approve of yourself. She recommends saying, "I approve of myself" 300 to 400 times a day. Then saying, in front of a mirror, every time you pass by, "I love myself, as I am." She recommends that you not let what you think are your shortcomings, stop you from accomplishing your goals. Instead, she tells us to push past the pain. Subsequently, she encourages you to behave in a way that fosters approval of self and talks about planting seeds of goodness and never stomping on someone's efforts.[320] If you are feeling pain and resistance, acknowledge it, but never allow yourself to stop moving toward your goal. Sometimes, maybe, many times, you must push aside your pain and continue to perform the needed actions to move toward your goal.

I highly recommend Hay's book, "You Can Heal Your Life," because when you approve of yourself, you can forgive others and yourself, all shortcomings and bring more peace and compassion to yourself and the world. Learning to let go of unresolved issues and conflicts you may have with others and yourself, leaves you with emotional energy to expend on important goals rather than nursing slights and outdated, unproductive feelings of unworthiness.

In my practice, I found as difficult as it was for some clients to forgive someone else when feeling wronged, it was sometimes much more difficult to forgive themselves for their past poor choices.

Seventeen

L et me take this opportunity to present some guidance to assist in awakening the Sleeping Tiger that resides within each of us. *Please do not accept inaction from yourself!* Whenever you are confronted with a problem, learn how to brainstorm solutions and perform positive action. Action eliminates anxiety.

Learn to leave your comfort zone and become comfortable in being uncomfortable. The world needs you. The community needs you. Disrupt your paradigm. Push yourself to exceed and surpass what you think may be the limits of your capabilities. Know that everyone encounters failure. If you fail at something, learn from the experience. One failure does not define you as a person. It certainly does not make you a failure. That one event you call a failure, can teach important lessons for your emotional and mental growth. It can become a valuable learning experience. Remember, Hertz said, "If you will it, it is no dream."[321] Muslims say, "If God wills it, it is no dream."

A. Guidance and Religion

What guidance can you turn to? For guidance, recommendations or direction to be complete, let us remember the role of religion and spirituality. Whatever your religious tenets, your religious text will help you keep God in mind and do good works for humanity.

The Quran teaches us that remembrance of God calms the soul.[322] Our youth need direction, not criticism from trusted adults. Sometimes the world provides you with excessive criticism; however, direction from holy books and books that offer guidance, principles and high values. For example, the Nahjul Balagah, (Peak of Eloquence) written by Imam Ali (the Prophet's son-in-law, philosopher, leader and warrior), is illuminating not only for Muslims but also for non-Muslims to read.

Islam transformed a society of pagans who were so immoral and brutal they buried their live daughters after birth. One man of moral virtue, Mohammed, changed the entire psychological dynamics of the Arabian Peninsula and the world. Do we have the will to work together to implement a strategy for long-term positive change? What is our vision?

The Quran was brought to humanity as a gift, not a criticism. It teaches a moral code. Does it teach us how to live when part of society is corrupt? It teaches that God has power over life and death and that we need two things for a good life and after life: first, to believe in God, and second, to do good deeds or positive action. We are told that if you can stop harmful actions toward the oppressed, then do so. If you cannot, then speak about it. If you cannot speak, due to oppression, then at least think and feel good intentions in your heart.

In my opinion, exclusively "talking" about events in Palestine, discrimination, or unfair stereotyping in or outside the U.S. does not meet God's expectations of us. Nor should it meet *our* expectations because we have power to create positive change. Certainly talking and translating talk into "positive action" would better meet our expectations.

Do you accept corruption in society or does it make you more determined to vote for fair and just representatives? Can you work toward removing the corrupt individuals from office? You have the option to either run for office or elect people who have open minds, seek the truth and will represent you in a just and balanced manner. Thus, seek knowledge so you can understand how to communicate your ideas in a logical manner and offer information to elected officials who may not have the knowledge, access or awareness of the issues that you do.

In the Quran, we are told that if we believe in one God and do good works, we can go to heaven, and that God wants to purify us. If we follow our religious tenets, we see that a person of any religion or without religion offers something to the world. It is my hope that you can learn to value each other and value yourself regardless of media stereotyping.

If someone does not treat you with respect, do not associate with that person, if you don't have to. If someone at work harasses you, inform your union or someone in management who may be supportive. If a neighbor is causing you major problems, then inform the police. The police are paid to protect you. Usually, if we are respectful to others, they will be respectful to us.

Islam teaches us to treat our neighbors well. That means to be respectful of them and others. If someone treats us well, we are to treat him or her better or just as well. However, first, we are to take the initiative to treat them well. Learn to be proactive and assertive, not passive. Confidence comes from being proactive and assertive.

More individuals from our communities need to become attorneys, journalists, attend film school, run for office, join civil rights organizations, collaborate with other groups, and develop think tanks.

In 2016, there were only two Muslims in the U.S. Congress and no U.S. Muslim Senators. We have some Muslim mayors, but need many more. The right wing militant Zionist machine does not want Muslims or Arabs to have any power to influence or have input in U.S. government because without as much U.S. financial and political support, right wing militants believe there would be a different Israel; an Israeli government that would have less power and domination.

Does it seem ironic that Israel can aspire to be a "Jewish State?" Does that mean only Jews can live there or are entitled to human rights? What happened to the sound bite, "Israel is the only Democracy in the Middle East?" In contrast, if a Muslim majority country attempted to oppress a minority religious group, it would be broadcast throughout the news media. (You can research for yourself how many Muslim organizations in Muslim-majority countries have been placed on the U.S. terrorist list.)

Hypocrisy and discriminatory acts are being committed against Muslims and other minority groups in this and other Western countries on a regular basis. There is one standard for Muslims and other politically underrepresented minority groups and another standard for politically represented groups.

Parents, in particular, have a difficult job. They aspire to raise their children with love and confidence and to teach them resilience, motivation, a sense of responsibility and direction, and to give back to their community. Children need to feel special, to be loved and cherished, to take pride in making contributions toward society, and to learn to respect and value others as well as themselves.

Talking to our children about their daily activities is not sufficient. It is important to have "emotional" talks and to be emotionally present for our children when with them. Discuss our children's feelings about their daily happenings, about different aspects of their life, current events, friends, education, future dreams, ideas, values and goals. Parents can emphasize values that matter; achieving excellence, purity internally and externally, working toward accomplishing goals, meeting their human potential and helping others. When a person helps others, that person is helping his or her own soul. All of these endeavors bring us closer to God and bring peace to ourselves. We can help each other and help our children feel special because they are truly a gift from God.

Part of having a responsibility to our community and the community at large, is to have higher expectations of ourselves, our children and others, and especially those chosen to represent us in public office.

A wealthy and well respected, elderly individual from our community once stated, "I regret spending my life focused on the accumulation of money. Instead, I should have focused more on helping my community."[323] Please remember that money is a means to a goal, not *the* goal. Accumulating wealth is desirable. What matters more is how you earn the money (legally) and the way you spend it. Please try to see the bigger perspective and you will not have regrets when you are elderly.

B. Connection to God or Spirituality

> *"Nothing hurts a good soul and
> the kind heart more
> than to live amongst people who
> can't understand it."* –
>
> IMAM ALI

In my view, ingrained in most of us is an aspiration to connect with God. We call this sense or feeling of connection with God "spirituality". We are told that when we think of God, we will have peace. We hear the word "peace" so often that it seems to have lost its significance. Do we know the true definition of peace? Reflect for a moment, to understand the meaning of the word.

In my life, I have been fortunate to have had three spiritual experiences that impacted me so strongly, they changed my life. The first and very personal experience taught me about unconditional love and gave me certainty that there is a compassionate God. When you read about the definition of unconditional love, you are left wanting. My understanding of unconditional love is a simultaneous feeling of acceptance, understanding, compassion, and feeling valued and special. It is having a deep conviction that a greater being permeates our soul. It is a deep and genuine feeling that someone is able to look into your soul and truly love you for who you are and because you exist. It is a feeling that you will never forget.

The second experience taught me about heaven, a place of beauty, purity, and praise for God. It was the concern and love of a beloved relative who was near death and wanted me to know she was going to heaven, in the care of God, and for me not to worry about her.

The third spiritual experience taught me about peace. This was a feeling of magnificent inner tranquility, permeating the entire atmosphere and being surrounded by serenity and peace, inside and outside. It was a feeling and perception that I never felt before. The closest I can attempt to explain this feeling is to compare the peacefulness of awakening after a relaxing night's sleep. This portrayal does not come close to describing the intensity of the feeling of my spiritual experience. I am offering you this description so you can measure it on a continuum to understand the meaning better. *Peace* is not only inner tranquility but also being surrounded by tranquility that seems to envelop you: the world stops its speedy pace and a serene calmness is present, both inside and outside of your body. The peace makes you want to be in the presence of the compassionate one who created it. This word "peace" is encompassed in the word "Islam" and how some Muslims and Jews greet one another.

In the Islamic religion, if one believes and performs deeds of righteousness, the Most Gracious, God, will bestow love upon us, and "Every soul will receive its reward by the measure of its endeavor." When you read the Quran, you understand that God gives you the best gift that one could bestow. God gives you the gift of mercy. We need God's mercy; we need to accept and love ourselves and be merciful toward ourselves and others. If we can forgive ourselves for shortcomings, it will help free our energy to work on developing our goodness and developing skills for the betterment of society. We will have the energy, determination, and courage to work with groups to develop creative ideas, foster creative thinking and perform positive action (good deeds) for your community. You can become model citizens and role models for those of all religious denominations.

Each time a Muslim prays, he or she is asking God's help, showing gratitude to God, and encountering and winning an internal struggle between good and evil. Prayer actually is protection for our soul. God gives us the strength to feel confident and not to allow anything or anyone to distract us from the right path. In prayer, we ask God to show and keep us on the right path. Praying to God gives us hope. We try not to allow our hearts to be troubled and we start each day affirming that God brings hope for the future.

Muslims believe that Prophet Mohammed was the founder and role model for Islam. Many people believe that Imam Hussain, son of Imam Ali and grandson of the Prophet Mohammed, protected Islam because he stood up to the tyrant, Yahzid, who proclaimed himself absolute monarch in Damascus in 600's A. D.[324] Yahzid was an alcoholic, adulterer, and mocked Islamic Law. His soldiers murdered Imam Hussain and 72 of his relatives at Karbala, Iraq. Imam Hussain was revered as the salvation of Islam not only because he stood up to the tyrant but also, because he showed future generations that Islam is based on morality, not tyranny.

If there is such a concept as an "Anti-God", I believe it is violence, harm to God's creatures, oppression, arrogance, an uncompassionate attitude, untruthfulness, a judgmental attitude, and rejection of others. These characteristics are the opposite of those God possesses or values.

One individual told me, "If someone chooses Islam, it means they cannot have fun." In contrast, Islam does not stop you from having fun. Fun just needs to be balanced with important priorities and happenings in life. Imam Ali said, "Being an aesthetic doesn't mean you can't own things. It means things don't own you."

Eighteen

Analysis of Strategic Patterns

I t has taken me years to write this book. Searching through
much information, and having a wonderful editorial advisor
has actually caused my thinking to evolve to a yet, more understanding place. I learned to be careful about making generaliza-
tions or overstating a case. I attempted to find the most reliable
sources of information and learned that these sources ranged
from having small discrepancies to large ones. So how does one
arrive at the truth?

In some cases, more than one citation is given for a particular piece of information, while in others the original
documents were searched such as the Report of the Secretary-
General on the UN Disengagement Observer Force, the U.S.
Congressional Record, and *Propaganda and War.*

A. Strategic Patterns

In trying to make sense of some of top tier media's attempts to demoralize Muslims and Arabs, I noticed a pattern: powerful Western governments or their satellites appear to have a plan or strategy (such as the British plan to dominate India in the 1800's), or the Yinon (Zionist) plan for dissolving Arab states written in the 1980's.

This pattern includes a powerful government's plan to capture oil reserves, natural resources and land expansion. Then, in alliance with leaders from other powerful Western governments and with their respective media's help, they begin to turn public opinion against the third world leader. The powerful Western leaders begin to call the third world country's leader dehumanizing names. For example, President Reagan called Gadhafi a "mad dog". Bush called Saddam Hussein an "evil man", and the U.S. State department, under Obama, called Assad a "terrorist". If the leader or leaders of the third world countries have voiced a dislike for Israeli policies, then this seems to hasten the downfall of their regimes.

In the cause of Colonialism, powerful governments and their media manipulate their citizens' emotions and opinions; in some cases, a "coalition of countries" is formed, which preferably includes some Arab countries for credibility. At that point, bombing the third world country commences. Troops sometimes invade the country until the "unpopular" leader is toppled and new pro-Western leadership, who has been previously selected and vetted by the powerful governments, takes power.

It appears that some version of this strategy is more often than not involved in the removing leaders in countries with desirable natural resources. If the U.S. administration and Israeli government have the same strategic goals and both can benefit and agree on this strategy regarding the country (as in Iraq), then the bombing begins almost immediately. However, if for some reason, the U.S. administration does not have the same strategic goal as Israel's government (as in Iran), then the Israeli government seems to do whatever it takes to convince the U.S. Congress to arrive at their viewpoint. One example is when the Israeli officials brought U.S. Congressmen to Israel in 2015, before the U.S. Congressional vote on the Iran Nuclear Deal. A U.S. intelligence official said Israel's pitch to U.S. lawmakers included questions such as: "How can we get your vote?" "What will it take?" (Israeli officials were referring to ways they could get U.S. Congressmen to vote against the Iran Nuclear Deal.)[325]

Another example of Israeli officials doing whatever it takes to achieve their objective is when Israel threatened the International Court. The court was preliminarily investigating Israel for alleged war crimes during its offensive on Gaza in 2014, which left over 2,400 people dead and over 500,000 homeless. In January, 2015, Israeli Foreign Minister, Avigdor Lieberman said, during an interview on Israel Radio "We will demand of our friends in Canada, in Australia and in Germany simply to stop funding it [the court]."[326]

In writing this book, I learned that **some people and countries have to play by all the rules, some people and countries have to play by some of the rules, and some people and countries play by NO rules.** In other words, **he who has the power makes the rules**. Behind every story is often another meaningful or profound story.

Case in point: one report, a policy document written for Netanyahu to use in Israel, formulated in 1996, seems to sum up, succinctly, the information this book is asking you to question. It was prepared by The Institute for Advanced Strategic and Political Studies' "Study Group on a New Israeli Strategy Toward 2000." The report is titled, "A Clean Break: A New Strategy for Securing the Realm". The key passages for a possible speech in this report were marked TEXT (t) while the body of the report was marked COMMENTARY (c). Each (t) or (c) will be identified as reference point. The report indicated that Israel should no longer give "land for peace" (t) and that the Israeli government will continue to work closely with Jordan and Turkey to destabilize "dangerous threats" (c).[327] It discussed securing the northern borders by striking Syrian military targets in Lebanon and if that was insufficient, "strike at select targets in Syria proper"(c). The article further stated, "Israel can 'parallel' Syria's behavior by establishing the precedent that Syrian territory is not immune to attacks emanating from Lebanon by Israeli proxy forces (c)."[328]

Concerning the Palestinian issue, the report discussed upholding the "right of hot pursuit" for "self-defense" into all

Palestinian areas (c) and indicated that Israel must make sure "that our friends across the Middle East never doubt the solidity or value of our friendship (t)."[329] The stated new agenda includes reestablishing "the principle of preemption, rather than retaliation alone" (c). (Preemption translates into preventing the enemy in anticipation, "before" they perform a harmful action.) One aspect of the report with which I agree, was the idea of the U.S. reducing economic aid and loan guarantees to Israel. At least one participant in the study group said Israel is mature enough to cut itself free and it will foster (Israeli) economic reform (c). No mention was made of reducing U.S. foreign military aid to Israel.

Reading this policy report, coalesced four facts described in earlier chapters of this book. It reminded me of many similarities between the participants' ideas and "demoralization" and the "divide and conquer" techniques, mentioned earlier. These techniques included the following: First, the British strategy to demoralize and dominate India in 1800's; which is similar to the contemporary strategy of "hot pursuit" in all Palestinian areas and goes beyond.

Second, Wolffsohn, at the 10th Zionist Congress in 1911, suggested using manipulation to convince the Turks that the Zionists were their best friends-- similar to the present day strategy of "let our friends never doubt the solidarity or value of our friendship".

Third, Kermit Roosevelt from the U.S. created chaos in Iran in 1953 because the British wanted power over Iranian oil. He used the divide and conquer technique by hiring mobs to fight each other in the same way that the report, "A Clean Break", used Jordan and Turkey against other Arab countries.

Fourth, and finally, the report mentioned using Israeli proxy forces to fight Israel's enemies. This is reminiscent to supporting the opposition as proxies in order to cause chaos by using divide and conquer in the Middle East. The ideas of "demoralization" and "divide and conquer" techniques are obviously not new; however, the fact that people continue to be deceived by these techniques seems difficult to understand.

Some ideas stated in the "Clean Break" report were distorted or inaccurate: For example, Syria's last war with Israel was over 30 years ago; the premise of Arabs as the "enemy" is an outdated and incorrect portrayal. In fact, Arabs are more "victims" in this policy strategy to create a new plan for the Middle East. Israel supports the opposition in some countries who kill and have caused the displacement of millions of people. This chaos causes hardship for not only for the people but also for the several countries, including European ones that are attempting to shelter them. Apparently, these actions are taken to carve up and control the Middle Eastern countries for the benefit of Israel's security. The irony is that Israel is already secure.

Whether information sounds logical or illogical, please look at the source and then investigate to find the truth. It is important to use multiple and diverse sources of information, with a trusted record of reporting and a reliable reputation in searching for the truth.

History will repeat itself unless we learn from it. The value of never giving up and of awakening the Sleeping Tiger within will guide us well. As you move forward, I would like you to remember a quote from the Quran: "Against Goliath and his hosts, they said, O our Lord! Shower on us the blessings of endurance and set our feet firm and help us against the disbelieving people."

Victory may not come in a year, a decade or even your lifetime, but as David overcame Goliath, and God gave David wisdom, knowledge and the Kingdom, God will also help you. God is gracious to all his creatures.

B. Perspective

As previously mentioned, many in top tier media create and engage in divisive reporting. Sensationalism sells and more importantly, some in control, apparently have a political agenda that supports taking Palestinian land and excluding Palestinians from the State of Israel. Many people in the U.S. do not know much about the Middle East. That is the reason they can be easily manipulated. Some others in the U.S. are conformists and the mainstream media counts on that. I have given you many examples that show how our history has been distorted by those who control the media—whether it is newspapers or modern electronic communication.

The alienation felt by Arab, Muslim, and other politically under-represented minority communities is not by accident.

When the media attacks and denigrates entire groups of people for the actions of a few, they are deliberately using this strategy for their own unjust purposes.

When Israel was first created, the founders did whatever was necessary to achieve their goals; this included oppressing others, breaking commitments to the British, and blowing up the King David Hotel with British inside. At that time, the U.S. protected Israel with foreign aid. This aid continues to grow at an ever increasing rate. The benefit of enormous amounts of U.S. foreign aid has enabled Israel to become the only nuclear power in the Middle East with more than enough destructive power to subdue any of the surrounding countries.

How does Israel continue to receive large sums of money from the U.S.? I believe that Israel benefits from the creation and maintenance of perpetual turmoil in the Middle East. Consequently, Israel can argue that their country is on the verge of being decimated by their enemies. The premise that Israel continues to need exorbitant amounts of foreign military and other aid from the U.S. is unnecessary and outdated especially given there is so much poverty in the U.S. We know this fact and so does the Israeli government.

If someone speaks negatively about Zionism or Israel, the pro-Israeli machine casts that person, not only as anti-Israel, but also as "racist," and "anti-Semitic"; these labels are clearly mean-spirited, dishonest and vindictive. This strategy is an attempt to put the person on the defensive, and to shut down and prevent the discussion of the truth. However, this strategy lacks credibility. If you think about it, this strategy (an ad hominem argument), attacks the *person* presenting the facts, instead of speaking about the *substance* of the issue.

Some who hold power positions in the U.S. are allies with the right wing militant Zionists and want to maintain the status quo. They believe they need to reduce freedom of speech on college campuses by calling any disagreement with Zionism "anti- Semitic" and foster implementing laws calling the BDS movement "anti- Semitic" and, therefore, against the law.

Hasbara is a term used by the Israeli government to describe efforts to explain government policies and promote Israel in the face of negative press and to counter what they see as delegitimization of Israel around the world.[330] Edward Said, according to Wikipedia, explained in his article, *Propaganda and War*[331] "Hasbara methods used during the Second Intifada included free trips for influential journalists, seminars for Jewish university students, invitations to Congressmen …donations for election campaigns, telling photographers and writers what to photograph or write about, lecture and concert tours…, and advertisements in the newspapers attacking Arabs and praising Israel."[332]

What Edward Said stated in *Propaganda and War* and published in Al-Ahram Weekly was, "Israel has poured hundreds of millions of dollars into Hasbara during the Second Intifada for seminars for Jewish university students who over a week in a secluded country estate can be primed to "defend" Israel on the campus, bombard Congressmen and women with invitations and visits, pamphlets and money for election campaigns, directing (or ...harassing...) photographers and writers of the current Intifada into producing certain images and not others, etc., make frequent references to the Holocaust and Israel's predicament today, and... attacking Arabs and praising Israel."[333]

According to Daoud Kuttab, an award winning Palestinian journalist, "Seconds after a pro-Palestine article in a respected media outlet appears, a swarm of opposing comments immediately responds to the piece on various websites. These commentators are paid individuals, often university students who are hired by the Prime Minister of Israel's office to respond quickly and fiercely to anyone daring to criticize Israel or its actions."[334]

How many countries in the world are so fearful and restrictive of ideas that differ with theirs? Do these students actually believe that Israel is in a fight for its existence? Look around and notice the vast power Israel has over the Middle Eastern region.

Another fund, Tikvah, is a generously endowed and promotes neoconservatism and political leverage under the guise of "Jewish Studies" at some top universities.[335] In Braiterman's 2011 article, the Chairman of the Board, (who also sits on the Board of American Enterprise Institute), in a round table talk at a panel discussion, stated, **"We look for leverage in almost everything that we do....the ability to influence the most important people and places**, be they readers of the best books and magazines or the very best students in the very best academic programs."[336] Does that sound like political leverage?

Israel does not need protection from U.S. freedom of speech laws nor should they be attempting to stifle freedom of speech on our college campuses and elsewhere. When the state of Israel was one year old, open debate was perceived as an existential threat; however, clearly this is no longer necessary or appropriate when Israel is 68 years old. If we use the metaphor of a child, the child needed its parent's protection when it was a baby. After more than six decades, however, that child, as well as a country, should be able to stand on its own, without heavy reliance on the parental U.S.

Instead of the U.S. government giving 30,000 pound bunker bombs to Israel so its government can cause greater devastation to other Middle East countries, why not take some of our tax payers' money and give foreign aid to other Middle Eastern countries to create jobs, infrastructure, and economic stability? This economic assistance could reduce discontent and give the people hope for the future. Also, in fairness, shouldn't the U.S. government consider providing Middle Eastern countries additional foreign military aid? Foreign aid is helping Jordan and Egypt continue to be allies of Israel. Wouldn't this positive approach work with other countries? (It worked when the U.S. government gave money to the Taliban in Afghanistan to stop attacking our troops.)

In 2015, Prime Minister Netanyahu of Israel attempted to pressure President Obama to use military force instead of pursuing a nuclear deal with Iran. Additionally, he delivered a speech to Congress on March 3, 2015 to pressure Congress to vote against the deal. Top tier news media in the U.S., gave much publicity to Netanyahu's speech. Five days later, however, on March 8, 2015, 30,000 to 50,000 people in Tel Aviv, Israel demonstrated against Netanyahu's policies. They demonstrated against his failed policies, the socioeconomic gaps and the deterioration of the relationship between the U.S. and Israel under Netanyahu's leadership.[337] Was his trip to the U.S. and speech to Congress meant to garner support for his upcoming election and to show the Israelis the amount of power he holds in the U.S.?

Unlike U.S. Congress exhibiting support for Netanyahu's speech in 2015, it is inspiring that many Jewish and Christian Americans, Israelis, as well as Jews from other countries, no longer engage in the group think of defending "Israel – right or wrong". More and more Jewish Americans and Israelis are vocal about their love of Israel, yet disapprove of the unjust treatment Palestinians receive in the occupied territories. Furthermore, these human rights activists do not want to displace Palestinians and do not want to build settlements on Palestinian land. In fact, some Jewish activists are quite vocal and participate in the BDS movement.

In 2016, some conscientious former members of the Israeli Defense Force (IDF) even offered tours of the West Bank to highlight the Palestinians' living conditions and their situation.

I highly recommend that Islamic, Jewish, Christian, and communities of faith and non-faith, work together for social justice, peace, equality, and brotherhood. In my view, there will be a sense of hope for a future when our diverse communities live and work toward peaceful coexistence with our brothers and sisters in humanity, connecting all nationalities, races and religions.

We have the right and duty to be proud of ourselves and our traditions. We need to take steps to empower ourselves and other marginalized groups by providing all with accurate information.

Although we may feel alone and isolated, know deep in our hearts, when we reflect, God and justice are with us. Have the courage and determination to never back down. Remember that we are people of substance. No one said it would be easy, but strive to be resilient. Know that we all aspire to be more than we are. If we are courageous and determined, we will achieve our goal. When things look darkest, hope and light will began to rise.

Unfair treatment of Palestinians can be compared to the biblical story of David and Goliath. The people of Gaza, without an air force, navy, and few weapons, stood up and resisted Israeli oppression, despite Israel's superior weaponry, missiles, and white phosphorous gas that burns and mutilates victims. If the Gazans overcame those odds, then each of us has much to learn about bravery, resilience and defiance in the face of injustice.

In the 600's A.D., when Hussain, Imam Ali's son, was in Karbala, Iraq, he spoke out against the murderous tyrant and challenged the people of the time, "Who can help me? Who can help me, help the orphans? Who can help me change the world? Who can help me change the system?"

Can we accept his challenge on behalf of the people of his time, or was he challenging the people of all time? Please accept the challenge to improve society. God gave us many wonderful attributes. Do not underestimate our ability to create positive change. Consider this quote:

> *"I learned from Hussain how to attain*
> *victory while being oppressed."*

> Mahatma Gandhi

Nineteen

WISDOM AND RECOMMENDATIONS FOR
BROADER ENGAGEMENT AND DIVERSITY

As I am near the end of this book, my closing thoughts will present some points of *wisdom* about how to live more peacefully in the world and additional *recommendations* to become more actively engaged in a diverse society.

A. Wisdom

One of our greatest gifts is the ability to think and to reflect; to use our minds creatively, to know the difference between right and wrong, and to control our impulses. All religious systems that call for purity in mind and body are essentially honoring these processes and principles. These principles give us the necessary conditions to think things through, to reflect, and the ability to seek the truth. If we use our greatest gift wisely, to seek the truth, it will positively impact our life and others.

Every life is precious. Our family is precious. Please make wise decisions and judgments in selecting your partner before marriage. The decision you make regarding mate selection will impact both your life and your children's lives. In most cases, divorce will hurt your children, emotionally.

Raise your children with love, emotional support and reinforcement. Teach your children to have confidence by asking for their input on decisions relating to them, so they can develop confidence in their decision making. When you are with them, be emotionally present and listen to their words, ideas, and questions. Give them much praise and focus on the positive, not the one thing your child did incorrectly. Your children are special, they are not perfect. Don't expect them to be. Hear what they have to say, uninterrupted, even when you disagree. Everyone makes mistakes. Children and adults deserve to be treated with respect and care. Attempt to keep your anxiety in check, so you can raise calm, confident children.

Some people use anger to get their way. Don't let their anger cause you to feel unsure about yourself and your purpose on earth. Some will make up lies, to feel superior or arrogant. Know that God loves those who worship him, not themselves.

Everyone has a dark side and a side that moves toward the light – the percentage of each, is what makes the difference.

Remember to judge a person on the basis of his or her character, not his or her religion. Time, honesty, and testing the relationship, in the bad times as well as good, will indicate who your friends really are. It is better to be alone than to be with an untrue "friend".

Education is the key to a life of independence, achievement, and success. Education gives financial security to help self and others in society. It also gives a thirst for knowledge and enduring, intellectual growth.

In Islam, moderation and balance are recommended in living this life and working toward the afterlife.[338] We have an obligation to work with others to help our fellow man. Is our materialism holding us back and making us afraid to speak out. Does our love of material supersede our love of mankind?

The prophets of Judaism, Christianity and Islam all brought the same message. The message is "Help your fellow oppressed man." Shouldn't we work together to do the same thing? Working together will have a positive impact on our life, the life of the oppressed and the world.

In keeping with moral values, the following acts should never be committed:

1. Never do anything to hurt yourself or others because this will also hurt your family, friends, and community. Islam and other religions forbid it. God created your mind and body. God is there for us. Why would you

want to hurt yourself when there are so many positive things you can accomplish in this world?

2. If you drink alcohol, take drugs, or become obese, you may think you are invincible and will not become addicted or suffer any consequence for this behavior. Every addict had that same thought. Each of these vices will take years from your life.

3. Never perform violent acts. Refer to reasons in #1.

The Quran says to those who strive to serve God, God will guide them, and God is with those who do good deeds.[339] This reduces the importance of comforts and the impact of misery in this life.[340] It helps to keep perspective.

As Hajj (holy pilgrimage to Mecca) for Muslims, pilgrimage of Jews to Jerusalem, and Catholic pilgrimage to the Holy Vatican are sacred journeys toward God, "life" itself can be perceived as a sacred journey toward God and the path of God. Consequently, God wants us to purify our bodies and mind in order to have a God centered life.

Please understand that although one may think we are the center of the universe, and in many cases, we are the center of *our* universe, God wants us to reflect and find him in nature, our children, animals, and our life. When we help humanity, animals, and other living things, we are finding God and the right path. With this emotional growth, we will rise to a higher plane of existence.

Anne Marie Ameri, Ph.D.

Many times in the Quran, God tells us to reflect on our environment, on this life and the next life. That said, the Quran, is a prophecy of victory. In the 600's A.D., there was no hope of triumph for the Romans, and they lost much of their territory to the Persians (who were fire-worshippers), the prophecy of a Roman victory in the Quran, was accompanied by the prophecy of victory of Muslims over their most formidable enemy, the Quraysh of Mecca. Victory was perceived as impossible. A narrative in the Quran explains the rise and fall of temporal power and the constant change brought to fulfill God's plan. The Quran tells us never to give up. Just because we don't see success in this life, doesn't mean success won't be forthcoming for future generations.

Muslims can visualize the mindset of Prophet Mohammed; that Christians, Muslims and Jews are one body, one community. Members of each religious community can take positive action to engage in religious practices, such as fasting along with members of other religious groups, during Ramadan, Lent, and Yom Kippur.

Spiritual gatherings can be held for Muslims, Christians and Jews who believe in One God and want to focus on doing good deeds. Each week a representative from one faith could perform a service for a cohesive community, and focus on performing good deeds or "service" for all our communities, working together, as one. Isn't this what a "universal and loving religion" would espouse? From reading and reflecting on the words of the Quran, it states that anyone can ask God for help in pardoning and reforming his or her ways and God will help. It also states that God sees the intention in a person's heart.

In the afterlife, Muslims believe that God will acknowledge any good an individual has performed on earth and purify those who did good deeds. The Islamic concept of heaven emphasizes closeness in the presence of God, forever. In order to go to heaven, the Quran states, one believes (in God) and does good deeds. But all judgments are up to God and God's forgiveness. It is my understanding that if one has rejected God's guidance and consistently performed evil, without asking for God's mercy, then perhaps that person causes his own torment and will know what it is like to be distant or rejected by God, in the afterlife. When someone you love does not return your feelings, it is your personal hell. Only God knows how long this rejection lasts. Each circumstance and situation is different. In this way, we created our own heaven or hell.

Prophet Mohammed stated, "Religion is another name for love." Also, one of the characteristics of God is "the Loving". Please remember, God can forgive anything. The Quran states that even if your sins are as big as the earth and you ask God for forgiveness, you can or will be forgiven.

"Stay united and victory will be yours."

—Habib Bourguiba, Former
President of Tunisia

In order to move from complacency to positive action, I ask that you read and consider implementing some of the following suggestions that you feel resonate within you. I have organized the following recommendations under the topics of individual and family, community, educational and professional, legal, social, spiritual, and political as a way to help you systematize these suggestions. Please read and ask how you can achieve your goals in each of these important areas.

B. Recommendations for Individuals and Families

1. Attempt to stop all criticism of yourself. Confidence comes through compassion, forgiveness, discipline, and determination. It also comes by succeeding and overcoming your challenges. Focus on this thought, "You need to build yourself up, not criticize yourself."

2. In order to succeed, look for self-validation instead of social validation. Remember, because someone tells you information does not necessarily mean it is true. Check it out. Be a critical thinker. Get proof before you believe any statement Or argument no matter how logical it might appear on the surface. Also analyze information to determine whether it is actually a fact or an opinion presented as a fact.

3. You know the propaganda machine's goal is to demoralize you and break your spirit; therefore, with God's

will and strength, condition your mental attitude to be resilient and defiant in the face of injustice.

4. Do not engage in short term pleasure such as drugs, drinking, impulsive sex, impulse spending, overeating to the detriment of your long term well-being. These may become addictive and negatively affect the dopamine level in the brain. Once you begin this cycle, one will feel the need to take more and more drugs of choice to feel pleasure. Normal events or activities will no longer provide pleasure. All one craves is that drink, drug, or sugar. The drugs will alter the brain regions that control judgment and decision making.[341]

5. Have self-compassion. When you feel depressed or worthless, ask yourself where those feelings are coming from. Be honest with yourself about their origin. Then challenge yourself and ask, "Am I really worthless?" The answer is "No", God values all of us and we are given the privilege of living on earth. All of us make mistakes but God is forgiving and merciful so stop battling yourself. Instead, open your heart, love yourself as you are, and begin to search for a wiser path. Start working to make a positive change in yourself and your community.

6. Ask for help when you need it from a person you trust and feel would have your best interests at heart.

7. Treat your neighbor with respect and kindness. Help your neighbor. Take the initiative to be kind and thoughtful. Don't wait for your neighbor to take the

initiative. When someone does a kind act toward you, do a kinder or at least, as kind act for them.

8. If you are depressed or thinking about giving up on your dreams and aspirations due to the immense frustration and pressure from propaganda, I tell you, "Never give up. Try even harder and you will succeed, God willing."

9. Understand that the only failure is in not trying. Know there is no such thing as a "loser" and the only time one feels like a loser is if he or she does not try.

10. Be passionate about something. Think about your goals and objectives and choose a plan to succeed. When passionate about a goal, one is willing to put forth dedication and effort into following one's dreams and reaching their goal.

11. Move out of your comfort zone and become more active by taking positive risks.

12. Develop strategies to move your vision forward.

13. Think BIG and BOLD. Brainstorm with yourself and others to make a small seed of an idea blossom into a big and bold specific plan. Your plan should be specific, measurable, and well-coordinated. When you have an idea, make it inspirational: your excitement and enthusiasm will transmit to others and inspire them to become excited. They will become attracted and happy to be part of your team. If your goals are well thought out and implemented, you are likely to attain them. If you want to be a doctor, don't settle for anything less.

Aim for positions of leadership even if they seem out of reach. Where there is a will, there is a way.

14. Teach resilience by modeling – by overcoming challenges. Express anxieties about pursuing a goal, but don't allow anxiety to paralyze or hinder you from pursuing your goal.

15. Visualize yourself as a motivational speaker. Write the positives about yourself. In another column, write the challenges you have encountered and how you overcame them.

16. Look for every opportunity to research more of the truth, to disseminate your knowledge, and to have a positive influence on those around you.

17. Put forth all your effort to be the best you can. Ask for help when you need it. Do not allow your ego to stop you. This is false pride. Be open to asking for the help you need, whether it is psychological, medical, educational, financial, or spiritual.

18. Be open to learning and engaging in new positive experiences.

19. Don't allow your unconscious mind to be your enemy. Not all people you meet will be your friends, nor will all the people you meet be your enemies. You will be your worst enemy, however, if you allow the negativity of remarks made in the media or by others to seep into your unconscious mind. If you do, you will sabotage yourself by thinking you are not good enough to try. All you need to do is try *hard*, expend the energy and you WILL achieve your goals. The chairman of my Ph.D. committee said,

"It is all a matter of time on task." He was correct. Put a specific time aside each day to meet your goals and, God willing, eventually you will achieve them.

20. Understand the importance of education. Students who need financial help can go online to learn about the procedures to contact organizations and to access applications to secure scholarships or financial aid.

21. Strong familial and community ties make you stronger by helping foster your national and religious identity. Research suggests that discrimination has less effect on an individual who is an active member of his or her community than one who is isolated.

C. Recommendations for Communities

1. Form support groups of parents and adults to help our youth when they need someone to speak on their behalf.

2. Help to create effective support systems and reporting mechanisms in the community to assist youth who feel isolated or vulnerable. Coordinate with schools and religious institutions to identify vulnerable individuals.

3. Teach debating skills and techniques to youth to empower them to stand up for their ideas, values, themselves, and others in the face of criticism.

4. Help each other through connections utilizing legal, ethical, and non-violent positive behavior. Have a vision and a plan.

5. Support each other, emotionally, spiritually, and professionally. Everyone needs moral support. Help each other find jobs, pursue higher education, and listen for other ways you can help your brothers and sisters in humanity.

6. Do not judge a person based on his or her religious, national, or political affiliation; give the individual a chance to exhibit his or her character and values, as each person is different than every other person.

7. Reach out to other communities and people of different religions and nationalities, in a respectful, engaging manner. Most likely, they will have differing opinions, but you can learn from them and they can learn from you. The struggles and stresses of others may differ from yours, but they are no less meaningful.

8. Help your broader community by participating in organizations that help those in need such as Habitat 4 Humanity. Collaborate with those who may share different beliefs including other political or religious groups and organizations. Look into organizations such as J-Street or Jewish Voice for Peace.

9. Get involved in community organizing and work on national, state and local elections. Associate with people from your community who have vision; run for mayor, state and U.S. Congress and Senate, so your community will be represented at all levels. It takes years to develop alliances necessary to run for political office. Be patient; start at the bottom and work your way up.

10. Unite with fellow Muslim and non-Muslim community members to show support both in happiness and tragedy. Show compassion by sending messages of support or by visiting mosques, houses of worship or fellow Muslims, etc. Coordinate and collaborate on a local, national, and international level. If you have an idea, coordinate with other people to improve and expand upon your idea.

11. Long term, develop a 24 hour crisis hotline to assist members of your community who are having emotional problems (depression, anger, feelings of despondency).

12. Develop a 24 hour crisis hotline for any person to call who is approached by a government agency such as the FBI and needs assistance.

13. Combine your financial and intellectual resources, your skills, and your talents. In the early 1900s, Herzl told the Jewish community to pool their resources to come up with $200,000,000. They did. Could we do that today?

D. Recommendations for Educational and Professional Action

1. If a student needs tutoring, seek free tutoring through organizations in your community, such as HYPE Athletics in Dearborn Heights and Westland.

2. U.S. Magistrate, Judge Mona Majzoub, of Lebanese and Muslim background, stated at a speech at Henry Ford College in Dearborn, Michigan, that she believes

"education" is the key. In her opinion, we must leave the village mentality and become inclusive by looking beyond our communities and becoming welcoming of diverse groups. She feels we should reach out to groups outside of our comfort zones and should speak thoughtfully and carefully. She stated that the best way to counteract the stereotype of "terrorist" accusation is simply to be a good citizen.[342]

3. Attend the best universities you can to attain the best education and possibilities for networking and your future profession. Make the most of your education wherever you are – focus on studies, join organizations and make an effort to form connections and networks which will help with your professional goals.

4. Consider professions involved in policy-making (regulations, rules, and procedures for governing the public).

5. Read and listen to inspirational speeches such as Gamal Abdul Nasser's of Egypt and President Habib Bourguiba's speech, of Tunisia delivered March 3, 1965 in Jericho, Palestine (in the Appendix). Please reflect on Bourguiba's encouraging speech to all Muslims and their leaders to become cohesive, to take small steps, to be patient and not to have an inferiority complex or a superiority complex; instead, use intelligence and reasoning.

6. Learn how to become financially stable. Seek advice from professionals if needed. If possible, try to help another individual complete his or her education.

E. Recommendations for Legal Action

1. When an organization commits a wrongdoing (an illegal act) against you or a member of your community, it is appropriate to file a lawsuit against that organization. If you do not have the money, there are organizations to assist you including the following: CAIR, Muslim Civil Liberties Union, American Civil Liberties Union, and Muslim Legal Fund of America. If individuals and organizations are spreading abusive and libelous messages pertaining to your community, these individuals and organizations should be held legally responsible. Here are two examples:

    A half-Jewish, half-Arab woman, Shoshana Hebshi, sued Frontier Airlines and Federal Law Enforcement after she was detained and strip-searched at Detroit Metropolitan Airport. She was seated near two Indian males who were reported by the plane's crew for suspicious behavior because they stayed in the bathroom for too long.[343]

    In another instance, McDonalds Restaurant in Dearborn was successfully sued for serving non-halal meat when it advertised that the meat was halal. These suits show companies there are consequences for wrongdoings to our community.

2. If you know a person, a so called, "friend", who plants an idea for violent or other illegal behavior in your or someone else's mind, it is imperative that you immediately become suspicious of this person. Turn this person

in to your local anti-Discrimination agency, local law enforcement agency or other community agency that is known to protect you. Anyone recommending a violent idea is not your friend. Two examples:

> First an FBI informant acted as if he was the best friend of the son of the man who ran a militia in Michigan. He was such a "good friend" the son had him stand up as best man in his wedding.
>
> The second example is an FBI informant who was such a "good friend" of an Imam from Detroit that he traveled with him to different states. This Imam was later set up and killed by the FBI and law enforcement.
>
> Please use critical thinking and know that whatever you do, someone is going to know about it, but God is always watching.

F. Recommendations for Social Action

1. Be Creative. Use art exhibits, create music, present musical performances, and produce and direct plays with social justice messages.
2. If someone makes a discriminatory remark against you, learn how to distance yourself so you do not respond like a deer in the headlights. Distance yourself so you

learn to respond as a scientist or anthropologist and interpret the event with no more emotion than you would if you were driving to a store and navigating traffic. You can get through it. Learn to navigate and figure out a well thought out non-emotional response to the verbal attack. Know how to respond in an appropriate manner and what to say. Having a prepared response is helpful. That response should be a balanced, appropriate response – not a response that is over the top, vulgar, or hostile. Do not bow to hatred. Respond with dignity and remember that you are an ambassador of your faith and culture and, therefore, you need to respond, appropriately.

3. Create policy statements and then follow them as much as possible, leaving room for flexibility.

G. Recommendations for a Spiritual Foundation

1. Have God as your foundation because if you have no foundation, then you are likely to turn to society as your foundation for acceptance. When you are focused on the goals of society instead of your own goals, you don't develop properly because your focus will be to cater to those who influence you at that time. You need to develop your own goals. If you allow society to do your thinking and tell you who to be and how to act, you become a chameleon instead of your true self.

2. Work toward unity across all religious, racial and nationalistic boundaries. Emphasize similarities and work toward common goals to develop a universal brotherhood.

H. Recommendations for Political Action

1. Write letters to the President, Senators, and Congressmen to make your voice heard.
2. After you develop political alliances, run for political office. The first time, be prepared to lose, but next time, be prepared to win.
3. Develop a think tank using inductive and deductive reasoning with smart and creative people. Make predictions on what events may happen in the future. Then think ahead to counteract and respond to the negative events. Think of the opponents' motivation and reasons behind campaigns. Ask yourselves about the goals of anti-Islamic groups. Take positive action to counteract their goals. Use benchmarks to set short and long term goals with time deadlines.
4. Some organizations within the U.S are against the oppressive Israeli treatment of Palestinians in the occupied territories. These include J Street, Jewish Voice for Peace, and Campaign to End the Occupation of Palestine among others. Some Campaigns call for divestment, boycott and sanctions of Israeli products, whose companies exploit the Palestinians in occupied

territories. Much credit should be given to these individuals and organized groups who may be pro-Israel yet against the occupation of Palestine. Groups and individuals may want to seek out these rational thinking and pro-peace and justice groups as potential partners to foster peace and justice in Palestine and Israel.

5. To nurture positive change, Noam Chomsky states, "Those who possess positive values need to become active, combine financial resources and expend an incredible amount of effort."[344] These communities can generate interest in creative projects and help one another by exhibiting compassion for others as well as for themselves. Chomsky believes that "Democracy and freedom are essential and recommends citizen-controlled media, which can inspire people toward a vision of fairness, justice, and truth."[345]

6. Connect to similar justice and conscientious thinking communities, nationally and internationally. It is our responsibility to reach out to these groups and individuals, to become allied with them, and to offer support, cooperation and friendship for their enlightened viewpoints, wisdom, and public actions.

7. Research the ideas that other communities are implementing or have implemented successfully. You don't need to reinvent the wheel.

8. Form an international group to compile information about the treatment of Muslims in their respective

countries. Then speak with governments (both nationally and internationally) to discuss ways to improve the treatment of Muslims within their respective countries.

Although all the previous recommendations are important for community survival, in my opinion, two are most significant for community betterment and growth: First, connect to similar communities, nationally and internationally. Second, work toward unity across all religious, racial and nationalistic lines emphasizing similarities and working toward common goals. When you think about it, isn't this the message brought by our prophets?

Afterward

Some who hold power in the U.S. and Israel use their intellect to satisfy their wants and needs for power, disregarding the human rights and justice for other groups. Their vision includes long term strategies to maintain their power. Within the U.S. and Israel, politically underrepresented minority groups are gaining in population. That means Latinos, African Americans and Muslims within the U.S. would be entitled, by law, to have a future impact on politics and policy through voting and possible future representation. Some who occupy the actual power positions feel threatened by this possibility. Therefore, they look for ways to develop and implement strategies to counteract the growing minority groups' potential power and maintain the status quo. This strategy includes: Voter suppression, War on Drugs, War on Terror, and reducing or stopping immigration of "the other". (One could say these are euphemisms to disrupt the African American, Latino and Arab/Muslim communities and their voting rights in the U.S.)

In Israel, the barrier wall inhibits many Palestinians from exercising their voting rights.

Those who advocate suppressing the rights of minority groups don't understand that they are espousing a short sighted strategy. Do you wonder if those who actually hold powerful positions in the U.S. are the same ones who have power in Israel or is it the other way around?

Do those who attempt to create an environment where Muslims, Arabs and other minority groups feel ashamed of themselves, using the technique termed "mirroring"? If these aggressors are honest with themselves and deeply reflect, do they actually feel ashamed of themselves and their actions?

Please sit with your intelligent friends, and determine the positive actions that need to be taken to counteract this infringement of our rights in the U.S. and the Palestinians' rights in Israel. By uniting together, we can accomplish anything. After reading this book, you now have a better awareness of the political challenges and you are AWAKENING. Now, it is up to you to take the next step.... May God guide you.

This author can be contacted at:
Guiding Perspectives
P.O. Box 2536
Dearborn, Michigan 48123

Appendix

Two Speeches

In this chapter, you find two inspirational *speeches* by world leaders that wonderfully and poignantly clarify some of the key points in this book, uniting with your brothers and sisters in humanity (not having an inferiority or a superiority complex) to make a positive difference in our world.

The first speech is the welcome by Former President John F. Kennedy to Habib Bourguiba. In May, 1961, the President of Tunisia, Bourguiba, was the first foreign head of state to come to the U.S. after J. F. Kennedy was elected President.

The second speech is by President Bourguiba of Tunisia in 1965, in Jericho, Palestine, speaking to Muslims and their leaders about the importance of unity.

Please read the two speeches for the wisdom they impart and please reflect on them. Both speeches offer wise words and enlightening advice.

A. Remarks by the Former President of the United States, J.F. Kennedy, to Welcome President Habib Bourguiba of Tunisia, May 3, 1961

It is a great pleasure for me as President of the United States and also as a citizen of our country to welcome the President of a friendly country and a distinguished world statesman.

Long before I occupied this present responsibility, I had become familiar with the long struggle in the life of President Bourguiba for his country's independence. He spent years in prison. He spent years in struggle. He is given, in his own country, the name of the Supreme Combatant, because he had one goal always in mind: the independence and freedom of his country.

And now that independence and freedom has been won, he has put before his people another goal, and that is to build a better life for themselves, to make it possible for all of the people of his country to share in a more fruitful and abundant existence.

I think that it's most proper that the first head of state to pay an official state visit to this country in this administration should be President Bourguiba.

We welcome him. I think he knows that the people of this country admire those who stand for principle, those who fight for freedom. We have among us to-day a man who has fought for freedom and fought for principle.

It is a great honor to welcome him to the United States.

B. Speech by Tunisian President Habib Bourguiba in Jericho, Palestine, to Unite Arabs and Muslims, March 3, 1965

Anne Marie Ameri, Ph.D.

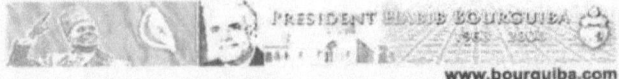

www.bourguiba.com

President Bourguiba
Jericho Speech (1965)

Jericho, March 3, 1965

Dear brothers,

I feel in this moment a double feeling of emotions and of pride. Moved, I am, when I think of the magnitude of the disaster that we underwent in Palestine seventeen years ago. However, at the same time, the enthusiasm that animates you, the savage will that I read on your faces, the determination to re-conquer your rights, all that comforts me and consolidates my optimism.

You undoubtedly know that while the Tunisian people carried out a rough fight against the most contemptible form of colonialism, still made a point of contributing its share in the war of Palestine. Of all the corners of Tunisia, young people and old men run here to take part with in the struggle whose stakes was assuring the integrity of Arab and Moslem land, which they regarded as their second fatherland. The Tunisian people managed, at the end of twenty-five years of fighting, to create a solid and modern State on a Muslim land, free of any Co-sovereignty and any form of political or military domination.

However, we think in Tunisia that our action is not circumscribed within our interior borders, Tunisia which fought colonialism is conscious of the role that it must play in the liberation of every inch of the Arab nation that remains under foreign grip. I have already proclaimed in the first Arab Summit conference, that Tunisia was decided to place at the disposal of the Palestinian cause all its potentialities. I proclaim it again today. It is however, a point to which I would like to draw your attention: you are the holders of a violated right; for this reason you owe to yourselves to be at the front line for the recon quest of Palestine. It is of my duty with all frankness to inform of certain number of truths, which you must keep present in mind: On the one hand, your role in the fight is of a primary importance. It is what you should never lose sight of. On the other hand, I would like to say, in this moment when I am addressing all the Arabs everywhere they are, that my personal experience, resulting through a hard and long fight, taught me that enthusiasm and passionate demonstrations of patriotism, are not enough to achieve victory. It is a necessary, but not sufficient condition. The spirit of sacrifice and contempt of death, one needs a lucid commandment and a thinking head that can organize the fight, see far, and anticipate the future. However, the rationally conceived struggle implies a precise knowledge of the adversary's mentality and an objective appreciation of the balance of powers so to avoid adventure and the useless risks which would worsen our situation.

1 / 4

262

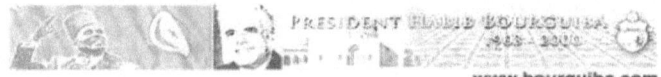

It is thus necessary to arm ourselves with lucidity, to work out our plans carefully and to create all the conditions of success. It is necessary to prepare the men and to equip them with proper means. It is also necessary to reinforce our fighting potential through the support of the international opinion. To avoid any precipitation dictated by passion, we need to act; with understanding in order to reach the goal, here is the essential.

When all these conditions are met, then our cause will triumph, more so because the Right is on our side. It is up to the people in charge to join the assets of success. We missed these assets when we had, a few years ago, engaged in the battle. This time, it is without respite that we need to work to join them together. We must benefit from the experiences and impose to ourselves hard reflexion effort. We are already on the right way; but the way is long. To reach the goal, our action requires loyalty, seriousness, and moral courage.

It is extremely easy to indulge in blazing and bombastic proclamations. In another way, it is just as difficult to act with method and in earnest. If it appears that our forces are not sufficient to destroy the enemy or to pare it out of our grounds, we would have no interest in ignoring it, or hiding it. It should be loudly proclaimed. Force is to us then to resort, at the same time as continues the fight, with the means that enable us to reinforce our potential and to bring us closer our objective by successive stages. The war is made of tricks and smoothness. The art of war is based on intelligence; it implies a strategy and a meticulously prepared process.

It does not matter that the way leading to the goal is direct or tortuous. The person in charge for the battle must insure the best route leading to the goal. Sometimes, requirements of the fight impose contours and turnings.

It is true that the mind accepts more easily of the straight line.

However when the leader see that this line does not lead to the goal, he must take a turning. The short-sighted militants could think that he gave up the pursuit of the goal. It is up to him to explain that this turning was intended to avoid the obstacle that could not be overcome in a direct way. Once the obstacle circumvented, the walk can resume on the main road to victory.

More than one Arab leader found himself in the impossibility to act in this manner. However, our defeat and the stoppage of our troops at the borders of Palestine prove the deficiency of our commanders. The impotence of the armies to deliver the victory despite the combatant's enthusiasm proves that the conditions for success were not gathered.

2 / 4

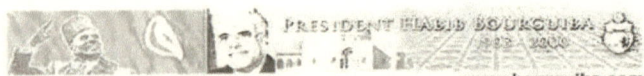

Today, the heads of states are seriously working to set up command that is at the level of its responsibilities. Nevertheless, that could not be enough. It is necessary that the people refrain from obstructing, by their passion overflows, their leaders' action. Their stubborn attachment to a certain policy should not put their political leaders in difficulty for executing their plans. We should not accuse of defeatism or of compromising any particular Arab leader, for his proposed partial or provisional solutions if these represent necessary stages on the way of the main objective.

For the people not to obstruct the execution of the agreed plans, it is necessary, as was the case in Tunisia that the people have confidence and rely on their leaders. It often happened to me to resort to the "policy of stages" when I found myself in the obligation to be the master of certain situations.

When certain militants showed reserves, I strove to convince them that my method could only lead to victory, especially when it appeared that our adversary showed some signs of weakness. It was then necessary to shake its positions of force, to affect its moral and to reinforce our position more at the same time.

As for the policy of the "whole or nothing", it brought us to the defeat in Palestine and reduced us to the sad situation we are struggling with today.

We would not have any way to succeed in Tunisia if we didn't abandoned this policy and accepted a step by step advance towards the objective. With each step, each conquest by the Tunisian people of a new strategic position, France yielded part of its privileges; for it was, the lesser evil for it. It then believed it had the capacity to stop the process. However, each conquered strategic point increased our leveraged more our means of action. The process became thus irreversible, step-by-step, France found itself driven back to the last battle, the battle of Bizerte where it could only yield finally.

In Palestine, on the contrary, the Arabs pushed away the compromise solutions. They refused the division and the clauses of the White Paper. They regretted it then.

If we had, in Tunisia refused in 1954, the internal autonomy as a compromise solution, the country would be have remained until this day under the French domination.

It is thus essential that the commander has the freedom of manoeuvre, is able to take any type of initiative, and should have some qualities of sincerity, probity, devotion, and perspicacity.

3 / 4

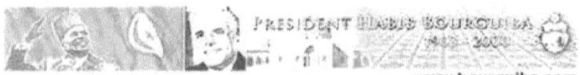

I made a point of coming and sharing with you this reflexion as a brother, broken for a long time with the anti colonial fight. I inculcated the concepts that I have just exposed you in your Tunisian brothers who ended up adhering to all my action plans.

They did sometimes feel uneasy though. Despite all this, they accepted to commit themselves under my impulse in such or such experiment because they already tested my devotion and my perspicacity. They noted the results. Today we are free and independent.

This is what a brother wanted to say in this occasion of my visit. Here is the advice that I believe is in my duty to give you and to all the Arabs. It is necessary to support the feelings and enthusiasm by a clear vision of the facts, so that our action could be effective.

I say it as a man who is completely disinterested, a man for whom you cannot dispute sincerity, nor the deep affection that he carries towards you.

We are reaching the goal. We will not spend seventeen or twenty years more deploring "the lost fatherland". To hold only to feelings would condemn us to live centuries in the same status. It would be the dead end.

From the Arab nation, voices must speak out to the people with frankness, knowing that the fight must continue with all it comprises in terms of turnings, steps, tricks until the day when we snatch a complete and final victory, not only for ourselves, but also for the future generations.

I ask of you to reflect on my proposal. Each one of us would have to be accountable before god and his conscience, for his deeds and intensions.

My dearest wish, is that the Muslims live within a very tight communion of hearts and that their leaders achieve among themselves a better understanding and fight all types of complexes: Inferiority complex with respect to an overestimated forces of the enemy, Superiority complex that might precipitate us into a surely avoidable catastrophe, thanks to unceasing recourse to the reason and to intelligence.

4 / 4

Endnotes

Memorial

1. Authorities investigate death of MIT grad student. (March 8, 2014). *Globe Newspaper Company*, copyright 2014. Cambridge, Mass. *www.Boston.com*.
2. State Officials release causes of graduate students deaths. (July 9, 2014). *The Tech,* online edition, Vol.134, Issue 29.*http://tech.mit.edu/V134/N29/causes.html*.

Chapter 1: Identity Theft

3. Noh, Samuel, & Kaspar, Violet. (February 2003). "Perceived Discrimination and Depression: Moderating Effects of Coping, Acculturation, and Ethnic Support." *American Journal of Public Health.* 93(2), 232-238.

Chapter 2: Propaganda

4. Lambert, Tim, A Brief History of India. *www.localhistories.org/india.html*.
5. Oren Liebermann and Salim Essaid.(August 1, 2015). Israeli police; Palestinian toddler killed, relatives injured in 'price tag' attack, *CNN.*
6. Haggai Matar, (November 28, 2015). Jews, Arabs march on Israeli checkpoint to demand an end to occupation, *+927 Magazine* (blog-based web magazine).

7.   Yael Marom, (January 15, 2016). Israeli, Palestinians march together against the occupation, *+927 Magazine*.

8.   Dolan, Matthew, Synder was late to learn about Flint's Legionnaires' outbreak. (March 18, 2016). Detroit Free Press, pg.5A.

9.   Chomsky, Noam, (Fall, 1993). "Early History of Propaganda, Spectator Democracy. Engineering Opinion. Public Relations". Excerpted from *Alternative Press Review*, MIT.

10.   Chomsky, Noam, Manufacturing Consent, *LinkTV*, March 19, 2013.

11.   Yazdi, A.A. H.M.M. P. and Ali, S.V.M. A., *The Holy Quran, Text, Translation and Commentary*, Introduction, pg. 122a and 123a.

12.   Weir, Alison, Against Our Better Judgment, The hidden history of how the U.S. was used to create Israel. (2014). Create Space Independent Publishing Platform, pg. 62-73.

13.   Howe, Russell Warren, "Fighting the 'Soldiers of Occupation' From WWII to the Intifada," in Seeing the Light: Personal Encounters with the Middle East and Islam, Ed. Richard H. Curtiss and Janet McMahon (1997). (Washington, D.C.: American Educational Trust), 38-39, in Weir, Alison, *Against Our Better Judgment, The hidden history of how the U.S. was used to create Israel*, Create Space Independent Publishing Platform, 2014, endnotes, pgs. 156-157.

14. Palestine 1946, King David Hotel Bomb Warning. *YouTube, www.youtube.com/watch?v=4ZHHTjuv5jc*

15. "Jewish Defense League". Southern Poverty Law Center. *www.splcenter.org/fighting-hate/extremist-files/group/jewish-defense-league.*

16. Carter, Jimmy, op-ed, "Reiterating the Keys to Peace", *Boston Globe*, (December 2006), from *Palestine Peace Not Apartheid*, Simon & Schuster, 2006.

17. Burke, Daniel, (April 3, 2015).The world's fastest-growing religion is ..., *CNN* Religion Editor.. *http://www.cnn.com/2015/04/02/living/pew-study-religion/*

Chapter 3: Accurate History of Islam: Dispelling Myths

18. Aslan, Reza, (2005). *No God But God*, Random House NY, NY. pg. 41.

19. *Merriam-Webster Dictionary*

20. *Merriam-Webster Dictionary*

21. Hass, Amira, (August 11, 2015). Israeli Colonialism, Plain and Simple, *Haaretz.*

22. Aslan, Reza, (2005), *No God But God*, Random House NY, NY. pg. 99.

23. The Presidency of Islamic Researches, IFTA, Call and Guidance, *The Holy Quran, English Translation of the Meaning and Commentary*, S. 10 A. 37.

24. Al-Ahzab *Quran*, Quran Commentary, 33:36.

25. Al-Ahzab *Quran*, Quran Commentary 33:36.

26. Aslan, Reza, (2005). *No God But God,* Random House, NY, NY. pg.80.
27. Parsons, Timothy, (2010). *The Rule of Empires*, Oxford University Press, N.Y., N.Y.
28. Bailey and Wise, (1969*). The First, Second, and Third Crusades-history of the Christian church.weebly.com/ the-first-second-andthirdcrusade.*
29. Personal communication with Kamran Pasha, April, 2013.
30. Bulliet, Richard, (1979). Conversion to Islam in the Medieval Period: An Essay in Quantitative History. *Harvard University Press*, MA., Pg. 33.
31. Parsons, Timothy, *The Rule of Empire*, Oxford University Press, N.Y., N.Y., pg. 96.
32. Abulafia, David, (2011). *The Great Sea,* Oxford University Press, Oxford, England.
33. *Enemy of the Reich: The Noor Inayat Khan Story,* Dir.and Prod. Robert Gardner, (2014) Unity Productions, Ca.
34. Francis: God wants to save everyone but the ruling class stands in his way. (Oct. 3, 2014). Vatican Insider, *La Stampa*.
35. Francis: God wants to save everyone but the ruling class stands in his way. (Oct. 3, 2014). Vatican Insider, *La Stampa*.

Chapter 5: Psychological and Physiological Warfare

36. Wolf, Paul, *Declassified CIA Document* Authority NND 877092 by JA NARA date (1/4/07).

37. Ibid.
38. El-Helah, Ahmed & Itani, Mariam. (2010). The Suffering of the Palestinian Child Under Israeli Occupation. *Al-Zaytouna Center for Studies and Consultations*. Beirut.
39. Concluding Observations of the United Nations Committee on the Rights of the Child, (June 2013).
40. Concluding Observations of the United Nations Human Rights Committee, (November, 2014).
41. Report by the *Universal Periodic Review*, (October, 2013). United Nations Human Rights Office of the High Commissioner. Media Brief.
42. Blumenthal, Terry and Kiang, Lisa, (June 2014). Research reported in *Monitor on Psychology*, Publication of the American Psychological Association, Washington, D.C., pg. 86.
43. Linkins, Jason. (July 17, 2012). "Michele Bachmann Points to Huma Abedin as Muslim Brotherhood Infiltrator." *Huffington Post*.
44. O'Keefe, Ed. (July 18, 2012). "John McCain defends Huma Abedin against accusations she's part of conspiracy." *Washington Post*.
45. White House Office of the Press Secretary. (August 10, 2012). "Remarks by the President at Iftar Dinner."

Chapter 6: How Our Youth Are Affected

46. Bail, Christopher, (December 21, 2014). *Terrified: How Anti-Muslim Fringe organizations Became Mainstream*. Princeton University Press.

47. https://en.wikipedia.org/wiki/Timothy_McVeigh
48. *http://www.breitbart.com/big-journalism/2010/10/25/ timothy-mcveigh-was-not-a-christian/*
49. Sugg, John, (January 1, 1999). *Steven Emerson's Crusade.* Fairness & Accuracy in Reporting. Jump up.
50. "48 Hours: Tracking Terror-Steve Emerson Watches Islamic Terrorist". (January 30, 2015). *CBS News.* Jump up.
51. *Al Jazeera,* (Published July 20, 2014). Al Jazeera Investigates Informants, Al Jazeera's Investigative Unit, www.youtube.com/watch?v=CMRns4ViuEY.
52. Ibid.
53. *Al Jazeera,* (Published July 20, 2014). Al Jazeera Investigates Informants, Al Jazeera's Investigative Unit, www.youtube.com/watch?v=CMRns4ViuEY.
54. Baldas, Tresa, (March 17, 2014) Detroit Free Press Staff Writer. Friends, Family doubt arrested Dearborn man was on way to join Hezbollah. *Detroit Free Press.* freep.com
55. Aaronson, Trevor. (2013) *The Terror Factory. Inside the FBI's Manufactured War on Terrorism,* Ig publishing, N.Y., N.Y.
56. Aaronson, Trevor. (2013). *The Terror Factory. Inside the FBI's Manufactured War* on *Terrorism,* Ig publishing, N.Y., N.Y.
57. http://www.salon.com/ (07/10/2013). only_1_percent_ of_terrorists_caught_by_fbi_are_real
58. Boston Marathon False Flag Proof? Finally Evidence of Conspiracy. www.youtube.com/watch?v=aXHIJQB0r9o April 22, 2013.

59. Boston Marathon False Flag Proof? Finally Evidence of Conspiracy. (April 22, 2013). www.youtube.com/watch?v=aXHIJQB0r9o

60. "Israeli police head to US to aid in Boston Marathon bombing investigation." (Apr, 17, 2013). *R T* Question More.

61. Boston Marathon False Flag Proof? Finally Evidence of Conspiracy. (April 22, 2013). www.youtube.com/watch?v=aXHIJQB0r9o

62. Boston Marathon bomber found guilty of all 30 charges. (April 8, 2015). *Fox CT* Staff, *Fox CT.*

63. Ellis, Ralph, (April 15, 2014).Lawyers say FBI tried to recruit brother of Boston Marathon bombing suspect. *CNN U.S.*

64. Turner, Lara, (April 9, 2015). Was Tamerlan Tsarnaev An FBI Informant? Odds say it's Possible. Who.What.Why.

65. Gessen, Masha, (April, 2015). *The Brothers: The Road to an American Tragedy.* Riverhead.

66. Ibid.

67. Friedemann, Karin, (Dec. 21-27, 2013). TMO, FBI Stalling Todashev Murder Investigations, *Muslim Observer,* Vol. 15, Issue 52, p.3 and 22.

68. Luscombe, Richard, (May 14, 2014). FBI agent cleared in killing of Boston suspect's friend had controversial past. *The Guardian.*

69. Ibid.

70. Gessen, Masha, (April, 2015). *The Brothers, The road to an American Tragedy.* Riverhead.

71. Lindorff, Dave, (March 24, 2014). Dark Questions about a Deadly FBI Interrogation in Orlando. *Counterpunch.*

72. Lindorff, Dave, (March 24, 2014). Dark Questions about a Deadly FBI Interrogation in Orlando. *Counterpunch.*

73. Friedemann, Karin, TMO, (Dec. 21-27, 2013). FBI Stalling Todashev Murder Investigations, *Muslim Observer,* Vol. 15, Issue 52, p.3 and 22.

74. Agent cleared. (March 22, 2014). *Detroit Free Press,* March 22, 2014, pg 2A.

75. Lindorff, Dave, (March 24, 2014).Dark Questions about a Deadly FBI Interrogation in Orlando. *Counterpunch.*

76. Gessen, Masha, (April 5, 2015). The Third Man. The Boston bombing, a triple murder, a mysterious death at the hands of the FBI, and the end of an American dream. Excerpt from *The brothers, the road to an American Tragedy.*Riverhead.

77. Ibid.

78. Lindorff, Dave, (March 24, 2014).Dark Questions about a Deadly FBI Interrogation in Orlando. *Counterpunch.*

79. Lindorff, Dave, (March 24, 2014). Dark Questions about a Deadly FBI Interrogation in Orlando. *Counterpunch.*

80. Personal communication from Najmeh Vahid Lahiji (March 13, 2014).

81. Copeland, Rick, (January/February 2014). *Medicaid Fraud Report,* pg 17-18.

82. Personal communication from Najmeh Vahid Lahiji, (March 13, 2014).

83.   Balko, Radley, (June 16, 2014). "Morning Links: Study finds rampant 'preemptive prosecution' in federal terrorism cases," *The Washington Post.* https://www.washingtonpost.com/news/the-watch/wp/2014/06/16/morning-links-study-finds-rampant-preemptive-prosecution-in-federal-terrorism-cases/ (cited September 29, 2015)

84.   Personal communication, from Najmeh Vahid Lahiji, on (March 13, 2014). Letter written for distribution.

85.   Henriques, Diana, (May 15, 2015) Bernie Madoff's Essential Man, *The New York Times Magazine.*

86.   Non-Muslims carried out more than 90% of all terrorist attacks in America. Terrorist Attacks on U.S. Soil by Group from 1980-2005. (January 24, 2015). *Global Research.* Princeton University's Loon Watch compiled chart from FBI data.

Chapter 7: Interaction Among Economics, Media and Government

87.   *https//en.wikipedia.org/wiki/trickle-down_economics*

88.   Dabla-Norris, Kochhar, Suphaphiphat, Ricka and Tsounta.(June, 2015).Causes and Consequences of Income Inequality: A Global Perspective. *IMF STAFF Discussion Note.*

89.   Dabla-Norris, Kochhar, Suphaphiphat, Ricka and Tsounta. (June, 2015). Causes and Consequences of Income

Inequality: A Global Perspective. *IMF STAFF Discussion Note.*

90. Lobe, Jim, (April, 2013). Israeli License to Cheney-Linked Energy Firm on Golan Heights Raises Eyebrows, *The Washington Report on Middle East Affairs*, Vol. XXXII, Washington, D.C. pg.32-33.

91. Lobe, Jim, (February 23, 2013). Israeli License to Cheney-Linked Energy Firm on Golan Heights Raises Eyebrows. *Inter Press Service,* Washington, D.C.

92. Grant, B., and Dawson, D. (Jan. 1998). Age at onset of alcohol use and its association with DSM-IV alcohol abuse and dependence: Results from the National Longitudinal Alcohol Epidemiologic Survey. *Journal of Substance Abuse*, Vol. 9, Pg. 103-110.

93. The Rohingya: The Most Persecuted people on Earth? (June 13, 2015). *The Economist,* from the print edition. *www.economist.com./.../21654124-Myanmars-muslim-mi.*

94. Iraqi Man killed in Dallas photographing snow. *www.cbsnews.com/...Iraqi-man-killed-in-dallas-photographing-snow-had-just-arrived.* (March 11, 2015).

95. *www.independent.co.uk/news/uk/home-news/britons-dislike-israel-more-than-iran--but-north-korea-beats-them-both-as-most-maligned-nation-10016643.html.*

96. Fletcher, Dan, (Feb. 20, 2009). A Brief History of the Fairness Doctrine. *Time Magazine.*

97. Fletcher, Dan, (Feb.20, 2009). A Brief History of the Fairness Doctrine. *Time Magazine.*

98. Ibid.

99. Who Owns the Media? *http://www.pbs.org/independent/ ens/democracyondeadline/mediaownership.html*

100. Sony CEO Michael Lynton slams Middle East leaked emails: "Let them all kill each other!" Chats with State Department. (April, 17, 2015).*WikiLeaks.*

101. Ibid.

102. Melman, Yossi, (November. 2013).   "Hollywood Producer was an Israeli nuclear agent." *Haaretz.com*, July 18, 20ll. *Detroit Free Press.*

103. Melman, Yossi, "Hollywood Producer was an Israeli nuclear agent." Haaretz.com, (July 18, 20ll). *Detroit Free Press*, Nov. 2013.

104. Melman, Yossi, "Hollywood Producer was an Israeli nuclear agent." Haaretz.com, (July 18, 2011). *Detroit Free Press*, Nov. 2013.

105. Said, Najla, (2013). *Looking for Palestine: Growing up confused in an Arab-American Family*, Riverhead Books, N.Y., N.Y., pg 123.

106. *Michigan.gov Press Release.* "Teacher tenure reform signed into law." (July 19, 2011).

107. Hefling, Kimberly. (June 12,2014). Some States Roll Back Teacher Tenure Protections. *HuffingtonPost.com*/2014/06/12/ states-eliminate-teacher-tenure_n_5488042.html.

108. Richmond, Todd. (January 18, 2013). "Scott Walker's Collective Bargaining Law Upheld by Federal Appeals Court." *Huffington Post.*

109. Cohn, Scott, (May 29, 2015). An American workplace war that's reached a tipping point. *CNBC.*

110. Cohn, Scott, (May 29, 2015). An American workplace war that's reached a tipping point. *CNBC*.

111. Borger, Julian, (September 26, 2013). Breakthrough hailed as U.S. and Iran sit down for nuclear deal discussion. *The Guardian*.

112. Reider, Dimi, (November 24, 2013).Iran nuclear deal poses a political challenge for Israel's Netanyahu. *CNN*.

113. Jordan, Will, Radhakrishnan, Rahul, (Feb. 23, 2015). Mossad contradicted Netanyahu on Iran Nuclear Programme, The Spy Cable, *Al Jazeera*, Investigative Unit.

114. Wong, Scott, (July28, 2015). Lawmakers to meet Netanyahu in Israel. *The Hill*, Washington, D.C.

115. Ibid.

116. General: Israelis exaggerated Iraq threat. *USAToday.com*. Posted December 12, 2003.

Chapter 8: The Cost of War Since 2001 and Cost of Aid
to Israel

117. Chantrill, Christopher, (Retrieved August 27, 2015).U.S. Federal Budget Analyst, U.S. Government Spending, *Budget of the U.S. Government* (Data Source), *usgovernmentspending.com*.

118. Molland, Judy. (Retrieved August 11, 2013).Care 2 Make a Difference: 5 Shameful Ways the United States is leading the World.

119. Terkel, Amanda, (June, 18, 2011). The War In Afghanistan: How Much Are You Paying? *The HuffingtonPost.com, Inc.*

120. Molland, Judy. (Retrieved: August 11, 2013). Care 2 Make a Difference: 5 Shameful Ways the United States is leading the World.

121. Trotta, Daniel, (Retrieved on August 22, 2015). Cost of war at least $3.7 trillion and counting. *Reuters.* New York.

122. American Public Opinion on U.S. Aid to Israel (PDF), by the Institute for Research: Middle Eastern Policy, *IRmep. P.R. Newswire*, September 30, 2014.

123. Zunes, Stephen, (January 26, 2015) The Strategic Functions of U.S. Aid to Israel, U.S. financial Aid to Israel: Figures, Facts, and Impact, *Washington Report on Middle East Affairs.*

124. Ibid.

125. Ibid.

126. Sharp, Jeremy. (June 10, 2015). *Congressional Research Service.* U.S. Foreign Aid to Israel.

127. Sharp, Jeremy. (June 10, 2015*). Congressional Research Service.* U.S. Foreign Aid to Israel.

128. Coren O., and Feldman, N. (March 20, 2013). U.S. Aid to Israel Total $233.7 Billion over Six Decades. *Haaretz.*

129. U.S. foreign aid to Israel: 2014, *Congressional Report.* (March 2, 2015). Journalist's Resource, Harvard Kennedy School, Shorenstein Center on Media, Politics & Public Policy.

130. Sharp, Jeremy. U.S. Foreign Aid to Israel. The Congressional Research Services Report, *CRS Report.* dated June 10, 2015, in If Americans Knew.org. Alison Weir.

131. Sharp, Jeremy. (April 11, 2013). Congressional Research Service. U.S. Foreign Aid to Israel.

132. *Iron Dome Support Act, H.R.1130,* 113th Congress, 1st Session, to authorize further assistance to Israel for the Iron Dome anti-missile defense system.

133. Sharp, Jeremy. (June, 10, 2015). Congressional Research Service. U.S. foreign Aid to Israel. *CRS Report.*

134. Ibid.

135. Sharp, Jeremy. (June, 10, 2015). Congressional Research Service. U.S. foreign Aid to Israel. *CRS Report.*

136. "To Curb Iran, should we give Israel Bunker Busters?" (April 8, 2014). *Washington Post.*

137. "It's Time to give Israel the Means to take out Iranian Nukes," (May 17, 2015). *New York Post.*

138. DSCA Transmittal 15-36, (May 19, 2015). Available online at:*[http://www.dsca.mil/major-arms-sales/israel-joint-direct-attack-munition-tail-kits-and-munitions].*

139. Poll: Most Americans oppose compensating Israel for Iran nuclear deal. Institute for Research: Middle Eastern Policy. (July 27, 2015). *PRNewswire-USNewswire..*

140. Weinger, Mackenzie. (August 11, 2011). "Report: 81 members of Congress to visit Israel." *Politico*, August 11, 2011.

141. Chehata, Hanan. (December 8, 2011). "Cynthia McKinney blames the pro-Israel lobby for ruining her political career." *Middle East Monitor.*

142. U.S. lawmakers forced to pledge loyalty to Israel. (April 25, 2015). *Live Leak.www.liveleak.com/view?i=6ab_1430012729.*

143. "John Bolton, the Media's Favorite Undisclosed Romney Advisor." (September 21, 2012). *Media Matters*.

144. Ambassador John Bolton Interview with Greta van Susteran, (July 24, 2012). *Fox News* "On the Record."

145. Ronen, Gil. "Bolton to Israel: Attack, it's your right." (August 31, 2012). Arutz Sheva Israel National News.

146. "Mitt Romney's Olympics blunder stuns No. 10 and hands gift to Obama." (July 26, 2012).*The Guardian UK*.

147. LaFranchi, Howard. "Mitt Romney in Jerusalem: Another city, another gaffe (or two)?" (July 30, 2012). *Christian Science Monitor*.

148. Grattan, C. Hartley, *Why We Fought*. (1969). The Bobbs-Merrill Company, Inc., N.Y., N.Y. pg. 50.

149. Grattan, C. Hartley, *Why We Fought*. (1969).The Bobbs-Merrill Company, Inc., N.Y., N.Y. pg. 50.

150. Butler, Judith. "Judith Butler's Remarks to Brooklyn College on BDS." (February 7, 2013).*The Nation*.

151. Ayyash, Samia. Dehumanizing the Palestinian cause on campus. (March 2-8, 2013). The Arab American News, 29, (1412), p.10. Reprinted from the Michigan Daily.

152. Ibid.

153. Ayyash, Samia. Dehumanizing the Palestinian cause on campus. (March 2-8, 2013). The Arab American News, 29, (1412), p.10. Reprinted from the Michigan Daily.

154. Hedges, Chris, Israel's War on American Universities, (March 17, 2014).TruthDig.com.

Chapter 9: Americans (Christians and Jews) and Israelis
Speak About Injustice

155. American Public Opinion on U.S. Aid to Israel (PDF), by the Institute for Research: Middle Eastern Policy, (September 30, 2014). *IRmep.* P.R. Newswire.

156. Israeli Nuclear Arsenal prohibits US Foreign Aid under Symington Amendment. (March 31, 2009). *PRNewswire-USNewswire.*

157. Birch, D. and Smith, R. Israel's Worst-Kept Secret. (September 16, 2014). *The Atlantic.*

158. Poll: Israel's nuclear weapons program should be acknowledged and inspected. (June 8, 2015). Institute for Research: Middle Eastern Policy. *PRNewswire-USNewswire.* Washington.

159. U.S. blocks nuclear disarmament move over Israel concerns. (May 23, 2015).
Times of Israel. AP and Times of Israel staff.

160. Poll: Israel's nuclear weapons program should be acknowledged and inspected.(June 8, 2015). Institute for Research: Middle Eastern Policy. *PRNewswire-USNewswire.* Washington.

161. http://www.israellobby.org/krytons/default.asp

162. Poverty rate rises in America. (September 13, 2011). *CNN.*

163. On Point with Tom Ashbrook. (June 25, 2013). *NPR*

164. Coleman-Jensen, Al, Rabbitt, M., Gregory, C., & Singh, A. Household Food Security in the United States in 2014. USDA ERS. In Feeding America. The

Impact of Hunger. Hunger and Poverty Facts. www.feedingamerica.org/hunger-in-America/impact-of-hunger/hunger-and-poverty/hunger-and-poverty-fact-sheet.html?

165. Todd, Jonathan, Finding Funding for Much-Needed Infrastructure Improvements. (February 6, 2015). *Urban Land, The Magazine Of The Urban Land Institute.*

166. Hanauer, Nick, "The Pitchforks are coming for Us Plutocrats." (July/August, 2014). *Politico Magazine.*

167. James, Brendan, Princeton Study: U.S. No Longer An Actual Democracy. (April 18, 2014). TPM, *Livewire,*

168. *The Gatekeepers. (2012).* Dror Moreh. Sony. Film.

169. *The Gatekeepers.(2012).* Dror Moreh. Sony. Film.

170. *The Gatekeepers.(2012.)* Dror Moreh. Sony. Film.

171. *The Gatekeepers.* (2012). Dror Moreh. Sony. Film.

172. *The Gatekeepers.(2012).* Dror Moreh. Sony. Film.

173. *The Gatekeepers.* (2012). Dror Moreh. Sony.Film.

174. Cook, Geoffrey. "As Obama Goes to Palestine." (February 22-28, 2013). *The Muslim Observer.* 15(9), pg. 2.

175. Cook, Geoffrey. "As Obama Goes to Palestine." (February 22-28, 2013)*The Muslim Observer.*15(9), pg. 2.

176. John, Robert, *Behind the Balfour Declaration, Britain's Great War Pledge to Lord Rothschild,* Institute for Historical Review, www.ihr.org/jhr/v06/v06p389_John.html

177. American Council for Judaism Website http://www.acjna.org/acjna/default.aspx

178. Brownfeld, Allan, (April, 2013).The American Council for Judaism: 70 years of Challenging Jewish Nationalism,

The Washington Report on Middle East Affairs, Vol. XXXII, No. 3,
Washington, DC.

179. Ibid.

180. Ibid.

181. Ibid.

182. Siegman, Henry, former executive director of the AJC, President of the U.S./Middle East Project. "Give up on Netanyahu, Go to United Nations." (shown August 13,2015).Interviewed by *AmyGoodmanToday*, Henry Siegman, Leading U.S. Jewish Voice for Peace: www.democracynow.org/2015/8/13/henry_siegman_ leading_us_jewish_voice#, taped May,2015.

183. Ibid.

184. Weiss, Rabbi Yisroel Dovid, (July 18, 2014) Jews United Against Zionism. Speech at the Islamic Center of America, Dearborn, Michigan, Presentation

185. Weiss, Rabbi Yisroel Dovid, (July 18, 2014) Jews United Against Zionism. Speech at the Islamic Center of America, Dearborn, MI. Presentation.

186. Shaikh, Nermeen.Interviewer on Amy Goodman Today. "Give up on Netanyahu, Go to UnitedNations." (August13, 2015).Henry Siegman, Leading U.S.Jewish Voice for Peace:DemocracyNow.*www.democracynow. org/2015/8/13/henry_siegman_leading_us_jewish_voice#.*

187. Central Rabbinical Congress. Central Rabbinical Congress Denounces Lobbying by Pro-Israel Groups Against Iran Deal. (August 27, 2015).*PRNewsire-USNewswire*, New York.

188. Leading Israeli journalist: Israel is an apartheid government. (August 22-28, 2015). *The Arab American News*. Vol. 31, Issue 1529.Detroit, Michigan. Pg.16. Chapter 11: International Issues.

Chapter 10: International Issues

189. Presentation at Islamic House of Wisdom (August 2012). See also "Life lessons from the people of Palestine." *Epistle Magazine*, Summer 2011, pg. 10-11. http://www.lstc.edu/media/pdf/epistle/2011-summer/epistle-magazine.pdf

190. Ibid.

191. Presentation at Islamic House of Wisdom, (August 2012).

192. 10 things to know before visiting Israel, the West Bank and Gaza. (September 11, 2013).
Matthew Teller, *CNN*.

193. Rosenberg, Oz. "Suspect involved in Jerusalem 'lynch' of Palestinian: 'Let him die, he's an Arab."(August 20, 2012). *Haaretz*.

194. Dalouche, Mohamed, (December, 2013). Facebook video.

195. Halaka, John, Presentation on Palestine. (October, 11, 2013). Arab American National Museum.

196. Ibid.

197. FIFA urged the ban of Israel over shooting of Palestinian boy footballers. (March 6, 2014). GM, *Reuters*.

198. Zirin, Dave, quoted in, Shooting Feet: Israel Targets Palestinian Soccer Players. (March 13, 2014). author Zimet, Abby, *Common Dreams*.

199. Following His Father, A Palestinian Hopes for Peace. (March 16, 2014). *NPR*. www.npr.org/.../following-his-father-a-palestinian-hopes-for-peace.

200. "Official: 5 Egypt police killed on Israeli border." (August 19, 2011). *AP*.

201. "Israel Apologizes for Deaths of Egyptian Troops in Shootout with Militants." (August 20, 2011). *CNN*, AP.

202. "Israel Apologizes for Deaths of Egyptian Troops in Shootout with Militants." (August 20, 2011). *CNN*, .AP

203. Marcus, Jonathan. Deaths as Israeli forces storm Gaza aid ship. (May 31, 2010). www.bbc.com/10195838.

204. Ravid, Barak, U.S. Senator seeks to cut aid to elite IDF Units operating in West Bank and Gaza, (Aug. 16, 2011). *Haaretz*. www.haaretz.com/u-s-senator-seeks-to-cut-aid-to-elite-idf-units-operating-in-west-bank-and-gaza-1.378800.

205. Ibid.

206. Lewis, Aidan, Profile Muammar Gaddafi. (June 27, 2011). *BBC News*.

207. Pecquet, Julian, Emails to Hillary contradict French tale on Libya war, *Al-Monitor,* Congress Pulse, www.almonitor.com/pulse/originals/2015/06/libya-gadhifi-french-spies-rebels-support.html#

208. Ibid.

209. Ibid.

210. NATO bombing of Libya led to Mediterranean migrant deaths. (April 20, 2015).

RT Question More,

Chapter 11: Decline of Empires and Empire Building

211. Augustine of Hippo, *Confessions*, (BK X, Ch. XXIII, 34)

212. Parsons, Timothy, <u>The Rule of Empires, Those who built them, Those Who Endured Them, and why they always Fall.</u> (2010). *Oxford University Press*, New York, New York.

213. Parsons, Timothy, <u>The Rule of Empires, Those who built them, Those Who Endured Them, and why they always Fall.</u> (2010). *Oxford University Press*, New York, New York.

214. Ibid.

215. www.Merriam-Webster.com/dictionary/Zionism

216. Naqavi, Ali. *Islam and Nationalism.* (1984). Islamic Propagation Organization. Tehran, Iran.

217. Naqavi, Ali. *Islam and Nationalism.* (1984). Islamic Propagation Organization. Tehran, Iran.

218. Ibid.

Chapter 12: Formation of Israel Beginning in
the 19th Century

219. Herzl, Theodor, *The Jewish State,* (1988). Dover Publications, Inc. New York.

220. Herzl, Theodor, *Old New Land,* (2012). USA, Lexington, Kentucky.

221. Herzl, Theodor, *The Jewish State,* (1988). Dover Publications, Inc. New York.

222. John, Robert, *Behind the Balfour Declaration, Britain's Great War Pledge to Lord Rothschild,* Institute for Historical Review, www.ihr.org/jhr/v06/v06p389_John.html

223. John, Robert, *Behind the Balfour Declaration, Britain's Great War Pledge to Lord Rothschild,* Institute for Historical Review, www.ihr.org/jhr/v06/v06p389_John.html

224. www.eurasiareview/com/21122011-republicans-want-jerusalem-herzl-promised-pope-kaiser-and-sultan-to-leave-it-outside-jewish-state-oped/

225. John, Robert, Full text of "Behind the Balfour Declaration-Britains Great War Pledge to Rothschild Bankers." (March 7, 1919). Institute for Historical Review, and in American Jewish News.

226. Ibid.

227. Kizzia, Tom. *Novel involving Alaska Jewish Colony is rooted in History,* Anchorage Daily News. http://www.and.com/news/alaska/story/8828757p-8729539c.html

228. Protocols of the 10th Zionist Congress, p.11, quoted in John, Robert, *Behind the Balfour Declaration: Britain's*

Great War Pledge to Lord Rothschild, Institute for Historical Review, www.ihr.org/jhr/v06/v06p389_John.html

229. Noor, Ismail, Ph.D. (March 23, 2013).Arab American National Museum, Dearborn, MI.

230. Bawardi, Hani, "From Syria to Michigan." Arab American National Museum. Dearborn, MI. Presentation.

231. Protocols of the 10th Zionist Congress, p.11, quoted in John, Robert, *Behind the Balfour Declaration: Britain's Great War Pledge to Lord Rothschild,* Institute for Historical Review, www.ihr.org/jhr/v06/v06p389_John.html

232. Protocols of the 11th Zionist Congress, p.6, quoted in John, Robert, *Behind the Balfour Declaration: Britain's Great War Pledge to Lord Rothschild,* Institute for Historical Review, www.ihr.org/jhr/v06/v06p389_John.html

233. Grattan, C. Hartley, Preface to Chaos, *War in the Making.* (1936). Dodge Publishing Company, N.Y., NY.

234. John, Robert, *Behind the Balfour Declaration, Britain's Great War Pledge to Lord Rothschild,* Institute for Historical Review, www.ihr.org/jhr/v06/v06p389_John.html

235. Retrieved from http://en.wikipedia.org/w/index.php?title=Sykes-Picot_Agreement&oldid=508163313

236. Kedourie, Elie. April 23, 1964. "Promises on Palestine (letter)". *The Times.* p. 13.

237. John, Robert, *Behind the Balfour Declaration, Britain's Great War Pledge to Lord Rothschild,* Institute for Historical Review, www.ihr.org/jhr/v06/v06p389_John.html

238. John, Robert, *Behind the Balfour Declaration, Britain's Great War Pledge to Lord Rothschild,* Institute for

Historical Review, www.ihr.org/jhr/v06/v06p389_John. html - US Ambassador Diary Entry

239. John, Robert, *Behind the Balfour Declaration, Britain's Great War Pledge to Lord Rothschild,* Institute for Historical Review, www.ihr.org/jhr/v06/v06p389_John. html - US Ambassador Diary Entry.

240. John, Robert, *Behind the Balfour Declaration, Britain's Great War Pledge to Lord Rothschild,* Institute for Historical Review, www.ihr.org/jhr/v06/v06p389_John. html - US Ambassador Diary Entry.

241. John, Robert, *Behind the Balfour Declaration, Britain's Great War Pledge to Lord Rothschild,* Institute for Historical Review, www.ihr.org/jhr/v06/v06p389_John.html

242. *Memoirs of Herbert Samuels.* (1945). Viscount.

243. John, Robert, *Behind the Balfour Declaration, Britain's Great War Pledge to Lord Rothschild,* Institute for Historical Review, www.ihr.org/jhr/v06/v06p389_John.html

244. John, Robert, *Behind the Balfour Declaration, Britain's Great War Pledge to Lord Rothschild,* Institute for Historical Review, www.ihr.org/jhr/v06/v06p389_John.html

245. John, Robert, *Behind the Balfour Declaration, Britain's Great War Pledge to Lord Rothschild,* Institute for Historical Review, www.ihr.org/jhr/v06/v06p389_John.html

246. Ibid.

247. John, Robert, *Behind the Balfour Declaration, Britain's Great War Pledge to Lord Rothschild,* Institute for Historical Review, www.ihr.org/jhr/v06/v06p389_John.html

248. Ibid.

249. Ibid.
250. Ibid.
251. Ibid.
252. Strom, Kevin, *Jewish Terror: The Story of Lord Northcliffe*. (Broadcast January 10, 2004). American Dissident Voices.
253. Bazian, Hatem, Lecture on Palestine. (July 11, 2015). Henry Ford Centennial Library.

Chapter 13: Outcome of Dividing Palestine to Become the State of Israel

254. Letter from Jubran Kuzma to Ameen Farah, Quoted in, *The Making of Arab Americans, From Syrian Nationalism to U.S. Citizenship.* (2014).Bawardi, Hani, University of Texas Press.
255. Sami Abu Shehadeh and Fadi Shbaytah, Jaffa: From Eminence to ethnic Cleansing. The Electronic Intifada, (February 26, 2009). In *al-Majdal, quarterly magazine* of the Badil Resource Center for Palalestinian Residency and Refugee Rights, Autumn 2008/Winter 2009.
256. Bawardi, Hani, From Syria to Michigan. (March 23, 2013). Arab American National Museum.
257. Documentary, The Birth of Israel (2008). *BBC.* shown on *Link TV,* 2014.
258. Shehadeh, Sami Abu and Shbaytah, Fadi, Jaffa: From Eminence to ethnic Cleansing. The Electronic Intifada. (February 26, 2009). In *al-Majdal, quarterly magazine* of the Badil Resource Center for Palestinian Residency and Refugee Rights, Autumn 2008/Winter 2009.

259. Documentary. *The Birth of Israel, BBC.* (2008). shown on *Link TV,* 2014.

260. Documentary. *The Birth of Israel, BBC.* (2008) shown on *Link TV,* 2014.

261. Palestinian terrorists inject Mercury into Israeli oranges; 5 Dutch children poisoned after eating them. (February 2, 1978). *Jewish Telegraphic Agency.*

262. Barghouthi, Mustafa, Secretary General, Palestinian National Initiative, (April 5, 2013). Presentation in Dearborn, MI.

Chapter 14: Empire Building From 1953

263. American Coup (A Documentary). (March 19, 2013). Link TV, (Ch 375), 7pm CET.

264. Ibid.

265. Ibid.

266. Molotsky, Irvin. Kermit Roosevelt, Leader of the C.I.A. Coup in Iran, Dies at 84. (June 11, 2000).*The New York Times,* N. Y., N. Y.

267. American Coup (A Documentary). (March 19, 2013). *Link TV,* (Ch 375), 7pm CET.

268. Kinzer, Stephen, *The Brothers: John Foster Dulles, Allen Dulles, and Their Secret World War* (2013). Times Books Henry Holt and Company, LLC, N.Y., N.Y., 2013.

269. American Coup (A Documentary). Link TV, (Ch 375), March 19, 2013, 7pm CET.

270. LaRosa, Benedict. *Democracy or Republic, which is it?* (1999). Self Published.

271. Ibid.

272. Ibid.

273. Lagon, Mark. "Promoting Democracy: The Whys and Hows for the United States and the International Community." (February 2011).*Council on Foreign Relations.*

274. Lagon, Mark. "Promoting Democracy: The Whys and Hows for the United States and the International Community." (February 2011). *Council on Foreign Relations.*

275. Tait, Robert. "Iran's Jews reject cash offer to move to Israel." (July 12, 2007). *Guardian UK.*

276. Israel hints that it was behind the Syria strike. (Feb. 4, 2013). *Detroit Free Press.* p. 5A.

277. After destroying 10,000 homes, Gaza can rebuild if it disarms. *Monodoweiss.net/2014/08.*

278. Hosenball, Mark. "Obama authorizes secret US support for Syrian rebels." (August 1, 2012). Reuters.

279. "Syria Conflict: UK to give extra £5m to opposition groups." (August 10, 2012). *BBC.*

280. "France gives non-lethal military aid to Syrian opposition: PM." (August 22, 2012). *Al-Arabiya.*

281. "UK and German spies feed intelligence to Syrian rebels—reports." (August 19, 2012). *http://rt.com/news/ uk-germany-intelligence-syria-054*

282. Adl-Tabatabai, Sean, IDF and Syrian Opposition Figures on Border. (February 11, 2015).
Your newswire.com, *Middle East News*.
283. Kazerooni, Ibrahim, Ramadan Lecture at the Islamic House of Wisdom. (July 11, 2015).
284. James Corbett Report, (Aug 30, 2013). http://www.corbettreport.com/?p=7893
285. Engdahl, F. William, James Corbett Report. (Aug, 30, 2013). *http://www.corbettreport.com/?p=7893*
286. Escobar, Peppy, James Corbett Report. (Aug, 30, 2013). *http://www.corbettreport.com/?p=7893*
287. Shahak, Israel,"Greater Israel". The Zionist Plan for the Middle East, The "Infamous Oded Yinon Plan", A Strategy for Israel in the Nineteen Eighties, Oded Yinon, Global Research, (4/29/13). AAUG, Inc. March 3, 2013.
288. Ibid.
289. Rasheed, Fayez, Has the "Greater Israel" project finished? (May 1, 2014). *Middle East Monitor,* Yariv Levin.
290. Russia is stopping USA's Secret Mideast strategy "Greater Israel", World Peace. (October 22, 2015).*https//www.youtube.com/watch?v=fllLK1sC4yk.*
291. Shahak, Israel, "Greater Israel". The Zionist Plan for the Middle East, The "Infamous Oded Yinon Plan", A Strategy for Israel in the Nineteen Eighties, Oded Yinon, *Global Research*, (4/29/13). AAUG, Inc. March 3, 2013.

292. Sniegoski, Stephen, (2008). *The Transparent Cabal: The Neoconservative Agenda, War in the Middle East, and the National Interest of Israel.* Norfolk, Va., Enigma Editions.

293. Haissam, Nabil. Plans to redraw the Middle East map are underway. (May 30-June 5, 2015). Commentary. *The Arab American News.* Detroit, Michigan.Vol.31. Issue1529. Pg 16.

294. Rasheed, Fayez, (May 1, 2014).Has the "Greater Israel" project finished? *Middle East Monitor,* Yariv Levin.

295. Adl-Tabatabai, Sean. UN: Proven ties Between ISIS and Israel. (February 11, 2015). *Your newswire.com.*

296. Downes, Nathaniel, U.N. Finds Credible Ties Between ISIS And Israeli Defense Forces. (February 5, 2015). *Addictinginfo.org.*

297. Report of the Secretary-General on the United Nations Disengagement Observer Force for the period from 20 November 2014 to 3 March 2015. (March 13, 2015). *United Nations Security Council,* S/2015/177.

298. Perkins, Robert, Under Fire, Israel's artillery policies scrutinized. Ed. Overton, Iain. (Dec. 2014). Research and Publication funded by the government of Norway, Minister of Foreign Affairs.

299. Report of the Secretary-General on the United Nations Disengagement Observer Force for the period from 20 November 2014 to 3 March 2015. (March 13, 2015). *United Nations Security Council,* S/2015/177.

300. Ibid.
301. Israeli Commanders Killed within Al Nusra Ranks inside Syria. (August 29, 2015).
Global Research-Center for Research on Globalization. *Fars News Agency.*
302. Israel Fuels The Syrian Crisis With Aid to Al-Qaida Rebels. (May 4, 2015). *Mint Press News*, Desk.
303. Salaheddin, Yacoub and Perry, Al Qaida Breakaway Declares Islamic State. (June 30, 2014). *The Detroit Free Press*, Associated Press. pg 2.
304. Syria's Kurds declare federal region. (March 18, 2016). Detroit Free Press. 2A.
305. U.S., Britain pull some staff from Yemen due to terror threat. (August 4, 2013). *CNN. www.cnn.com/2013/08/06/politics/terror-threats/.*
306. Quick Hits, "Attack in Yemen." (August 11, 2013). *Detroit Free Press.* 2A.
307. Drones Team, Bureau of Investigative Journalism. (July-Aug., 2013).Get the data: Drone Wars Yemen Reported U.S. covert actions.
308. Brumfield, B. and Liebermann, O. Leaked audio: Israeli leaders drew up plans to attack Iranian Military. (August 22, 2015). *CNN.*
309. Cohen, Moshe, and Liberman: Disloyal Arab-Israelis should be beheaded. (March 8, 2015).
Arutz Sheva 7, *IsraelNationalnews.com.*
310. Israeli Commanders Killed within Al Nusra Ranks inside Syria. (August 29, 2015).

Global Research-Center for Research on Globalization. *Fars News Agency.*

311. AP. "NSA privacy rules broken thousands of times, Edward Snowden leaks documents show." (August 21, 2013).*Telegraph UK.*

312. All nations collect intelligence.*www.cnn.com/2013/07/01/world/Europe/eu-nsa/*

313. Shoichet, Catherine, Bolivia: Presidential plane force to land after false rumors of Snowden on board. (July 3, 2013). *CNN. www.cnn.com/2013/07/02/world/bolivia-presidential-plane.*

314. *www.aljazeera.com/indepth/features/2013/07/201371 0113522489801.html*

Chapter 15: Historic Treatment of Racial Groups and "Outgroups"

315. Beaumont, Peter, Leaders reject Netanyahu calls for Jewish Mass Migration to Israel.
(Feb.16, 2015). *The Guardian.*

316. Liebermann, O. and Conlon, K,. Protest over police brutality in Israel turns violent. (May 4, 2015). *CNN.com.* www.cnn.com/2015/05/03/world/israel-police-protests/.

317. Kershner, I. and Rudoren, J. Soldier becomes Unlikely Face of Ethiopian-Israeli Discontent. (May 4, 2015). *The New York Times.*

318. Gisolfi, Monica, Columbia University, Columbia American History on Line, (2004).

Columbia University, Digital Knowledge Venture, Slavery and the U.S. Constitution.

319. Abel, Jaison and Deitz, Richard, Do the Benefits of college still outweigh the costs? Current Issues in Economics and Finance, Vol. 20, Number 3, 2014, pg. 4. Federal Reserve Bank of N.Y.*www.newyorkfed.org/research/current_issues*.

Chapter 16: Accept the Challenge

320. Hay, Louise, *"You Can Heal Your Life"*. (2004). NY, NY. Hay House, Inc.,

Chapter 17: Guidance and Spirituality

321. Herzl, Theodor, Wiki quote, *https://en.wikiquote.org/wiki/Theodor_Herzl*

322. *Quran,* English Translation. (1411 H.). King Fahd Holy Quran Printing Complex.

323. Anonymous

324. Zakir, *"Tears &Tributes"*, (2004). Ansariyan Publications, Islamic Republic of Iran, pg.xi.

Chapter 18: Analysis of Strategic Patterns

325. Entous, Adam, and Yadron, Danny. (December 30, 2015). U.S. Spying Nabs Allies. *The Wall Street Journal*, NY., NY.

326. Nevins, Sean, (February 9, 2015). Israel Threatens Int'l Court With Retribution If War Crime Investigations Continue,). *Mint Press News.*

327. Perle, Richard. (1996). American Enterprise Institute, Study Group Leader, "A Clean Break: A New Strategy for Securing the Realm". Report prepared by The Institute for Advanced Strategic and Political Studies' "Study Group on a New Israeli Strategy Toward 2000." Information Clearing House.

328. Ibid.

329. Ibid.

330. Hasbara, Public diplomacy (Israel). Wikipedia.

331. Edward Said on Propaganda and War. "Hasbara" (January 27, 2007). Newsgroups.Derkeiler.com.

332. Said, Edward. Propaganda and War. (August 31, 2001)Media Monitors Network. Mediamonitors.net. Retrieved April 9, 2016 from Wikipedia.

333. Said, Edward. (August 30-September 5, 2001). War and Propaganda, Al-Ahram Weekly Online, Issue No. 549.

334. Kuttab, Daoud. (July 6, 2015). How to Counter Israel's Hasbara Campaign. The Palestinian reality does not welcome any serious media effort to counter Israel's Hasbara campaign. Al Jazeera News. Opinion.

335. Braiterman, Zachary, (September 6, 2011). Conservative Money and Jewish Studies: Investigating the Tikvah Fund. The Religious Case for Equality. ZEEK, first on-line Jewish magazine.

336. Ibid.

337. Harris-Gershon, David, Netanyahu govt. more 'frightening' than all Israel enemies. (March 8, 2015.) ex-Mossad chief tells crowds, *RT News*.

Chapter 19: Wisdom and Recommendations for Broader
Engagement and Diversity

338. *Quran.* Text, Translation, and Commentary by Ayatulla Agha Haji Mirza Mahdi Pooya Yazdi and S.V. Mir Ahmed Ali. 5th U.S. ed. (2005). Tahrike Tarsile Quran, Inc., Elmhurst, NY.

339. *Quran* 29:69. Text, Translation, and Commentary by Ayatulla Agha Haji Mirza Mahdi Pooya Yazdi and S.V. Mir Ahmed Ali. 5th U.S. ed. (2005). Tahrike Tarsile Quran, Inc., Elmhurst, NY.

340. Commentary *Quran* 29:64. Text, Translation, and Commentary by Ayatulla Agha Haji Mirza Mahdi Pooya Yazdi and S.V. Mir Ahmed Ali. 5th U.S. ed. (2005). NY: Tahrike Tarsile Quran, Inc., Elmhurst.

341. Volkow, Nora, Addiction and the Brain's Pleasure pathway: Beyond Willpower, *HBO/Addiction*: Understanding Addiction. Video and Article.

342. Majzoub, Mona, U.S. Magistrate Judge, Presentation, "Through My Eyes...The Arab American Journey," (March 22, 2013). Henry Ford College, Dearborn, Mi.

343. 'Half-Arab, Half-Jewish' Ohio woman 'was ordered to strip, bend over and cough' after she was pulled off a

plane in handcuffs along with two Indian men. (Jan. 22, 2013). *Daily Mail UK. http://www.dailymail.co.uk/news/article-2266667/*

344. Chomsky, Noam, *"Manufacturing Consent"*, (March 19, 2013).

345. Chomsky, Noam, *"Manufacturing Consent"*, (March 19, 2013).

www.ingramcontent.com/pod-product-compliance
Lightning Source LLC
Chambersburg PA
CBHW030419290526
45786CB00001B/54